NARRATIVE INQUIRY IN LANGUAGE TEACHING AND LEARNING RESEARCH

Narrative Inquiry in Language Teaching and Learning Research provides an entry-level introduction to narrative inquiry methods – research methods that involve the use of stories as data or as a means of presenting findings – that is based on the sociological and psychological literature, but is grounded in published empirical research within the field of language teaching and learning. It discusses basic definitions and concepts in narrative inquiry, explains how and why narrative methods have been used in language teaching and learning research, and outlines the different approaches and topics covered by this research. It also examines the different ways of eliciting, analyzing, and presenting narrative inquiry data. Narrative inquiry offers exciting prospects for language teaching and learning research and this book is the first focused and practical guide for readers who are interested in understanding or carrying out narrative studies.

Gary Barkhuizen is Associate Professor in the Department of Applied Language Studies and Linguistics at The University of Auckland.

Phil Benson is Professor in the Department of Linguistics and Modern Language Studies at The Hong Kong Institute of Education.

Alice Chik is Assistant Professor in the Department of English at the City University of Hong Kong.

Second Language Acquisition Research Series:
Theoretical and Methodological Issues
Susan M. Gass and Alison Mackey, Editors

Monographs on Theoretical Issues:

Schachter/Gass Second Language Classroom Research: Issues and Opportunities (1996)

Birdsong Second Language Acquisition and the Critical Period Hypotheses (1999)

Ohta Second Language Acquisition Processes in the Classroom: Learning Japanese (2001)

Major Foreign Accent: Ontogeny and Phylogeny of Second Language Phonology (2001)

VanPatten Processing Instruction: Theory, Research, and Commentary (2003)

VanPatten/Williams/Rott/Overstreet Form-Meaning Connections in Second Language Acquisition (2004)

Bardovi-Harlig/Hartford Interlanguage Pragmatics: Exploring Institutional Talk (2005)

Dörnyei The Psychology of the Language Learner: Individual Differences in Second Language Acquisition (2005)

Long Problems in SLA (2007)

VanPatten/Williams Theories in Second Language Acquisition (2007)

Ortega/Byrnes The Longitudinal Study of Advanced L2 Capacities (2008)

Liceras/Zobl/Goodluck The Role of Formal Features in Second Language Acquisition (2008)

Philp/Adams/Iwashita Peer Interaction and Second Language Learning (2013)

Monographs on Research Methodology:

Tarone/Gass/Cohen Research Methodology in Second Language Acquisition (1994)

Yule Referential Communication Tasks (1997)

Gass/Mackey Stimulated Recall Methodology in Second Language Research (2000)

Markee Conversation Analysis (2000)

Gass/Mackey Data Elicitation for Second and Foreign Language Research (2007)

Duff Case Study Research in Applied Linguistics (2007)

McDonough/Trofimovich Using Priming Methods in Second Language Research (2008)

Larson-Hall A Guide to Doing Statistics in Second Language Research Using SPSS (2009)

Dörnyei/Taguchi Questionnaires in Second Language Research: Construction, Administration, and Processing, Second Edition (2009)

Bowles The Think-Aloud Controversy in Second Language Research (2010)

Jiang Conducting Reaction Time Research for Second Language Studies (2011)

Barkhuizen/Benson/Chik Narrative Inquiry in Language Teaching and Learning Research (2013)

Of Related Interest:

Gass Input, Interaction, and the Second Language Learner (1997)

Gass/Sorace/Selinker Second Language Learning Data Analysis, Second Edition (1998)

Mackey/Gass Second Language Research: Methodology and Design (2005)

Gass/Selinker Second Language Acquisition: An Introductory Course, Third Edition (2008)

NARRATIVE INQUIRY IN LANGUAGE TEACHING AND LEARNING RESEARCH

Gary Barkhuizen, Phil Benson, and Alice Chik

Routledge
Taylor & Francis Group

NEW YORK AND LONDON

First published 2014
by Routledge
711 Third Avenue, New York, NY 10017

and by Routledge
2 Park Square, Milton Park, Abingdon, Oxon OX14 4RN

Routledge is an imprint of the Taylor & Francis Group, an informa business

Library of Congress Cataloging-in-Publication Data

Barkhuizen, Gary Patrick, editor of compilation.
  Narrative inquiry in language teaching and learning research /
Gary Barkhuizen, Phil Benson, Alice Chik; University of Auckland,
Hong Kong Institute of Education, and City University of Hong Kong,
    pages cm.—(Second Language Acquisition Research series)
  Includes bibliographical references and index.
  1. Language and languages—Study and teaching—Research. 2. Second
language acquisition—Research. 3. Discourse analysis (Narrative).
4. Linguistic analysis (Linguistics). I. Benson, Phil, 1955–editor of
compilation. II. Chik, Alice. III. Title.
  P53.27.N37 2013
  418.0071—dc23
  2013019226

ISBN: 978-0-415-50933-6 (hbk)
ISBN: 978-0-415-50934-3 (pbk)
ISBN: 978-0-203-12499-4 (ebk)

Typeset in Bembo
by Apex CoVantage, LLC

CONTENTS

INTRODUCTION

The use of narratives in research is nothing new. In the field of psychology, Sigmund Freud, who is said to have been an enthusiastic reader of Sherlock Holmes detective stories, used narrative case studies extensively in his work (Brooks, 1979). In the field of sociology, the Chicago School announced its presence in 1919 with a volume that begins with a powerful argument for the use of individual biographies in the investigation of social conditions, followed by an individual biography of a Polish peasant (Thomas and Znaniecki, 1919). Towards the end of the 20th century, however, when language teaching and learning research began to incorporate psychological and sociological approaches, these fields had come under the sway of experimental and statistical survey methodologies. It is only very recently, therefore, following a resurgence of interest in narrative in the social sciences that narrative inquiry began to take its place in the panoply of approaches to research that are now available to language teaching and learning researchers.

Our interests in narrative inquiry developed separately from each other at a time when few narrative studies of language teaching and learning had been published. We drew on psychological and sociological research, as well as emerging research in the field of education, both for our basic understanding of narrative inquiry and for our detailed understanding of methods of data collection and analysis. Although we were not aware of it at the time, others were doing much the same thing and we welcomed each new study with enthusiasm as it appeared. Eventually, we began to explore issues in narrative inquiry for language teaching and learning together through several collaborations. At the same time, the rate at which new narrative studies were published began to accelerate to the point where narrative inquiry could be considered an established approach to qualitative research in our field. The driving force behind this book is the belief that there is now a "critical mass" of narrative research in the field of language teaching and learning itself on which to build a manual of narrative research methodology that is specific to this field. This is not to say that we encourage readers to ignore work in other fields, but rather that we encourage exploration of the ways in which this work has been contextualized within and is exemplified by research on language teaching and learning.

The aim of this book is to offer advice on data collection and analysis to researchers who are interested in experimenting with narrative research. In this respect, this is a conventional "research manual." At the same time, we have adopted an innovative approach in basing this advice on a database of more than 175 published studies, from which we draw examples of how language teaching and learning researchers have used narrative inquiry to address specific issues in specific contexts of research. This means that, instead of beginning from general principles, we begin from concrete examples in an attempt to show how narratives are actually used, rather than explain how they should be used, to address issues of language teaching and learning. While we do offer general advice from time to time, we also encourage a situated and experimental approach to narrative research, which is, in fact, the approach that is most characteristic of published research to date. A narrative research journey is not a matter of following a set of cut and dried directions, but of feeling one's way through a project with the guidance of those who have gone before. By mapping out approaches and methods that have been used in published work on language teaching and learning to date, we hope to make that journey a little less unpredictable.

The picture of narrative inquiry in language teaching and learning that has emerged during the writing of this book has turned out to be complex, involving two major uses of narratives (*investigating* narratives and *writing* narratives), two directions of approach (through the *content* and *discourse* of narrative), and a variety of methods of collecting and analyzing data. In order to make sense of this complexity, we begin with an overview of narrative inquiry approaches both outside and inside the field of language teaching and learning research (Chapter 1). In the next three chapters, we deal separately with three major approaches to collecting data for narrative studies: orally (Chapter 2), in writing (Chapter 3), and in multimodal form (Chapter 4). Like all divisions in research, these are a matter of convenience and we note here that there is a certain bias towards the kinds of projects in which researchers collect original data from other people ("biographical" or "third-person" studies). Investigation of published accounts of language learning and "autobiographical" or "first-person" reflection are two important approaches to narrative inquiry that are not discussed in these chapters, because in these approaches the real work tends to begin at the point of analysis.

The last two chapters of the book deal separately with data analysis (Chapter 5) and reporting narrative studies (Chapter 6). In these chapters we are again concerned with the full range of data types and with a variety of analytical and reporting strategies. These chapters cover thematic and discourse approaches to analyzing narrative data and the use of narrative writing as a strategy for analyzing non-narrative data and presenting findings.

This book is intended to be read not so much as a set of guidelines to be followed, but as a map that we hope will help readers find their own ways through the rather complex terrain of narrative inquiry in language teaching and learning research. There are a good number of summaries of published studies scattered throughout the book. We have selected these papers because they exemplify particular approaches to methodology and we encourage readers to follow them up by reading the original papers. There is no single way of carrying out a narrative inquiry study and, indeed, it seems that each new study brings with it a new approach. In our view, this is all to the good and we hope that readers will feel inspired to add not only to the quantity of narrative studies in our field, but also to the variety of approaches available to us.

1

NARRATIVE INQUIRY IN APPLIED LINGUISTICS

1.1 The Narrative Turn in the Social Sciences

Jerome Bruner, one of the founding fathers of narrative inquiry, writes of two basic modes of thought, each providing a distinctive way of ordering experience. "A good story and a well-formed argument are different natural kinds," he writes, and both can be convincing in their own ways (1986: 11). Arguments convince of their "truth," appealing to procedures for establishing formal and empirical proof; stories convince of their "lifelikeness," appealing more to criteria of verisimilitude. Of these two modes of thought—Bruner calls them "paradigmatic" and "narrative"—the second is both older and more deeply rooted in everyday thinking; telling stories about past events is both a "universal human activity" (Riessman, 1993: 3) and "the primary form by which human experience is made meaningful" (Polkinghorne, 1988: 1). The paradigmatic mode of thought is more recent and associated with development of rational thinking. It is a widely held view that research is a way of producing and distributing knowledge that favors rational argument over narrative. In recent years, however, more and more social science researchers have questioned this view, suggesting that paradigmatic thought can lead to conclusions that are divorced from the lived reality of phenomena and conveyed through academic forms of writing that fail to convince, precisely because they lack the quality of lifelikeness that we expect of a good story.

In light of this critique, the social sciences have witnessed what has sometimes been called a "narrative turn." Narrative has become both a legitimate mode of thinking and writing in research and the focal point of a variety of approaches that come under the heading of "narrative inquiry." Narrative inquiry is both complementary to experiment, observation, survey, and other research methods, and an "alternative paradigm for social research" (Lieblich, Tuval-Mashiach and

Zilber, 1998: 1). As this book aims to provide a concise account of the practicalities of using narratives in language teaching and learning research, we refer readers to other sources for more detailed discussion of their use in the social sciences (Bruner, 1990; Lieblich, et al., 1998; Polkinghorne, 1988; Riessman, 1993, 2008). In brief, the main strength of narrative inquiry lies in its focus on how people use stories to make sense of their experiences in areas of inquiry where it is important to understand phenomena from the perspectives of those who experience them. Lieblich, et al. (1998: 7) write of two major interests in the field of psychology: predicting and controlling human behavior, and exploring and understanding individuals' inner worlds. One of the best ways of learning about individuals' inner worlds, they suggest, is through "verbal accounts and stories presented by individual narrators about their lives and their experienced reality." In the field of sociology, narratives have been seen as a means of investigating social phenomena from the perspective of "the changing experiences and outlooks of individuals in their everyday lives" (Roberts, 2002: 1). In the field of education, narrative inquiry has proved especially fruitful in the study of teachers' professional lives and careers (Bathmaker and Harnett, 2010; Clandinin and Connelly, 2000; Goodson and Sikes, 2001; Loughran and Russell, 2002; Webster and Mertova, 2007). Narrative is, in fact, part and parcel of research in many fields of inquiry, but we mention psychology, sociology, and education here, because language is, perhaps, best understood as a psychological, social, and educational phenomenon. Narrative inquiry is relevant to research in our field because it helps us to understand the inner mental worlds of language teachers and learners and the nature of language teaching and learning as social and educational activity.

But if narrative inquiry has much to contribute, why have we only recently come to realize its value? Four main explanations for the narrative turn in the social sciences have been offered. First, narrative inquiry has an intuitive appeal to researchers who have "become weary of variables and the quantification of the positivistic approach" (Josselson, 1993: xv). This explanation situates narrative inquiry within a broader turn towards qualitative research and points to a weakening of the assumption that psychological, social, and educational phenomena should be investigated in much the same way that scientists investigate natural phenomena. Second, interest in narratives reflects post-modern concerns with the self, identity, and individuality, arising from what Casey (1995: 216) calls a kind of "cultural vertigo" that is the consequence of "individuals vacating established social constructions of reality." This explanation situates narrative inquiry within a broader turn away from the quest for "grand" social theories that would enable social scientists to predict human behavior. A third, and related, explanation points to the importance that narrative has acquired in post-modernity as a resource that individuals draw upon in the construction of social identities (Giddens, 1991). From this perspective, self-narratives, or the stories people tell about themselves, help us to understand the ways in which individuals situate themselves and their activities in the world. Lastly, interest in narrative has been linked to a turn towards the idea that research should both involve and empower the groups and individuals whose behaviors are the subject of research. Narrative inquiry expands the range of voices that are heard in research reports, often highlighting the experiences of marginalized groups outside the academy, although we should always bear in mind the ways in which these voices are mediated through those of the researcher in published work (Casey, 1995: 215).

No doubt there are other explanations for the rise of narrative inquiry, but for the moment let us stick to these four and ask about their implications for our own field. Are you more convinced by a richly described individual case study than you are by statistical analysis of experimental data collected from large numbers of people? Do you believe that we can best understand the social forces that condition language teaching and learning behavior by understanding how individuals interpret and respond to them? Would you like research to tell us more about the meanings that individuals attach to teaching and learning languages and the consequences that teaching and learning have for their lives? Would you like to hear more about the diversity of language teaching and learning experiences through the words of teachers and learners themselves? If you answer "yes" to these questions, then you are likely to be interested in narrative inquiry as an approach to language teaching and learning research. You may also be interested in narrative inquiry because it is a profoundly human way of carrying out research; it gets you out of the house or office and into the real world of teachers, learners, and the stories they have to tell.

1.2 What is Narrative Inquiry?

A fairy tale is a story and a person who tells a fairy tale is a storyteller, but fairy tales are not research. The same may be said of stories about language teaching or learning, although here the issue is more complicated because much depends on how the stories are produced and what we can learn from them. Narrative inquiry brings storytelling and research together either by using stories as research data or by using storytelling as a tool for data analysis or presentation of findings. Narrative inquiry is an established umbrella term for research involving stories; *Narrative Inquiry* is also the title of the major cross-disciplinary journal in the field. Narrative research and narrative study are sometimes used as alternative terms. In this book, however, two closely related terms—"narrative analysis" and "analysis of narratives"—will be used to refer to a basic distinction within narrative inquiry. Following Polkinghorne (1995), "analysis of narratives" refers to research in which stories are used as data, while "narrative analysis" refers to research in which storytelling is used as a means of analyzing data and presenting findings. Gao's (2010) study of the published memoirs of a disabled Chinese language learner is a good example of "analysis of narratives." In this case the narratives that serve as data are published, but researchers may also elicit spoken, written, or multimodal narratives directly from teachers and learners, and subject them to further analysis. Wette and Barkhuizen's (2009) study of the curriculum challenges facing university English teachers in China is an example of an analysis of narratives study based on elicited written data. In "narrative analysis" researchers use narrative writing as a method of turning non-narrative data into stories in order to convey their understanding of the meaning of the data. Ó'Mochain's (2006) study of his attempt to address queer issues in an EFL course in a Japanese women's college draws on a variety of data sources but is reported in the form of a narrative. A second basic distinction concerns the relationship between researchers and participants in narrative research, for which we use the terms "biographical" and "autobiographical." In biographical approaches, the researchers analyze or tell participants' stories; in autobiographical research, they analyze or tell their own stories. These terms also delineate more specialized approaches within the broad field of narrative inquiry; in addition to "biographical research" (Chamberlayne, et al., 2000; Roberts, 2002), we have approaches such as "life history" (Bertaux, 1981; Goodson and Sikes, 2001), "life story" (Atkinson, 1998), and "oral history" research (Thompson, 2000); in addition to "autobiographical" research (Brock-meier and Carbaugh, 2001; Fivush and Haden, 2003), we have "autoethnography" (Ellis and Bochner, 2000), "personal experience" (Clandinin and Connelly, 1994), and "self-study" (Loughran and Russell, 2002). Recognizing that the distinction between biography and autobiography is often blurred in research, Benson (2004) uses the term "(auto)biographical" to describe research that involves either, or both, third-person and first-person data and methods. One source of confusion lies in the fact that the data used in biographical studies are often autobiographical from the participants' perspective. We would, for example, describe Gao's study of language memoirs as "biographical," although the data that he analyzes is auto-biographical (Gao, 2010). The distinction between biography and autobiography, therefore, is related more to the roles of researchers, who either study other people (biographically) or themselves (autobiographically). The waters are muddied in studies where stories are "co-constructed" by the researchers and the participants. This may be true to some degree of all narrative analysis studies in which the researchers work with participants to construct stories that emerge in the course of the research (Barkhuizen, 2011). The word "participant" is used here, therefore, simply to identify the person whose experiences are narrated in a study (either biographically or autobiographically), in work in which relationships between subjects and researchers often turn out to be highly complex: for example, in papers where participants are listed alongside researchers as co-authors (Murray and Kojima, 2007; So and Dominguez, 2004) or in multi-voiced papers such as Benson, Chik, and Lim (2003), which includes autobiographical writing and both autobiographical and biographical analysis.

A third distinction that we find helpful concerns the focus of narrative inquiry: Are we interested in narrative itself or are we more interested in the content of narratives? There is now a great deal of research on the language, discourse, structure, and sociolinguistics of narratives, which is less concerned with what narrators say than with how they say it (e.g., De Fina and Georgakopoulou, 2012; Ochs and Capps, 2001; Norrick, 2000; Thornborrow and Coates, 2005; Toolan, 2001). There is also a good deal of research that is more concerned with what narrators have to say about the topics of their stories, including most psychological and sociological narrative studies, which focus on what narratives tell us either about the people who tell them, or about the situations and events they narrate. Because this book is mainly concerned with narrative inquiry as a resource for research on language teaching and learning, it is also mainly concerned with narrative content. We cannot ignore research on the language and discourse of narrative, however, because it has strong implications for the limits of what we can say about the content of narratives. In particular, there have been criticisms of the reliance on narrative content (or what are often called 'big stories') in narrative inquiry, which argue that when we study narratives, "we are neither accessing speakers' past experiences, nor their reflections on their past experiences (and through them how they reflect their selves)" (Bamberg, 2007: 144; Stokoe and Edwards, 2007; Vásquez, 2011). The 'small stories' perspective that these critics advocate focuses instead on the stories that people tell in the course of everyday conversation, or "how selves and identities are '*done*' in interactions . . . interactions in which narratives are made use of" (Bamberg, 2006: 146).

This is a complex issue that we will return to when we discuss methods of data analysis in Chapter 5, but for the present, we note our own view that there is a good deal to be learned from narratives of language teaching and learning, provided we are sensitive to "the interpretive nature of narration" (Pavlenko, 2007: 169) and do not fall into the trap of treating narratives as factual accounts of their subject matter. If a participant tells us, for example, that her school language classes were dull and uninspiring, we must treat the comment as a subjective interpretation of what the classes were like and not as an objective fact. We will also need to ask whether there was a particular reason why the participant described the classes in this way to us, the researchers, in the particular context in which the data were collected. The problem here, perhaps, is to understand exactly what narratives represent. In psychological research, narratives are often seen as a key to understanding the ways in which individuals organize their experiences and the identities through which they represent them to themselves and others. In sociological approaches such as oral history, narratives offer alternative perspectives to official or academic accounts of historical events and often uncover issues that had not previously been visible. We argue that, as long as we guard against the risk of treating narratives as offering access to the "truth" about language teaching and learning, they have very much the same potential. Narrative inquiry can help us to understand how language teachers and learners organize their experiences and identities and represent them to themselves and to others. In a field that very often favors abstract, theoretical understanding of processes over the particular, contextualized knowledge of participants (Firth and Wagner, 1997), it can also help us to understand language teaching and learning from the perspectives of teachers and learners. In this sense, a focus on narrative content can certainly contribute to a richer and more rounded understanding of language teaching and learning as lived experience.

1.3 What are Narratives of Language Teaching and Learning?

Peter Medgyes's (1994) book, *The Non-native Teacher*, is fascinating both for its insights into the experiences of non-native English-speaking teachers (NNESTs) and for the author's frequent use of narratives. Like most academic books, it relies mostly on paradigmatic argument, but the argument is also punctuated by short narratives that add a great deal to its force. Medgyes begins the book with this short narrative of his life as a learner and teacher of English:

> I am a native speaker of Hungarian. I am a non-native speaker of English. I use Hungarian at home and English at work. I thoroughly enjoy this double life.
>
> I first encountered the English language at the age of five, in a private kindergarten where we learnt a few English nursery songs. I never learnt English at school, nor was it possible in Hungary for a long time, but I always had a private English tutor. At the age of nine, I announced that I was fed up with piano lessons. My parents agreed to let me stop, but only if I promised never to give up on English. It was a deal.
>
> I studied English language and literature at university. I had three outstanding professors, who spoke beautiful English too. And all three of them had learnt it *in Hungary*. Then I did my teaching practice—it was love at first sight and proved to be a lasting affair too. I was a school teacher for fifteen years and since then I have been a teacher trainer.
>
> (Medgyes, 1994: v)

Later, a suggestion that there is a tendency for culture to become less language-specific and more country-specific is illustrated by the following story:

> Recently, I spent some time in England. At a party, I talked to an American colleague about the linguistic and cultural deficit of non-NESTs. She said that despite being a native speaker, she would often feel excluded in the company of Brits. As fate would have it, a few minutes later conversation took a sudden turn around the dinner-table. I was rapidly losing my bearings. Catching my eye, the American whispered to me: 'This is it. I don't have the faintest idea what they are talking about, either!'
>
> (Medgyes, 1994: 61)

These are good examples of narratives of language teaching and learning and we will use them to begin to get to grips with what we mean by narratives in this context.

First, Medgyes's stories illustrate a number of general features of narratives. We can see, for example, that narratives:

- are spoken or written texts
- are produced by people who have something to tell
- are situated in time and space
- involve development over time
- have structures that correspond to the developments they describe
- encapsulate a point that the narrator wants to get across
- have purpose and meaning within the context of their telling.

In addition, narratives usually have a topic that is somewhat larger than the particular point that the narrator makes. The point of Medgyes's second narrative, for example, is to show how native and non-native speakers share certain difficulties when participating in conversation in unfamiliar cultural environments. But in the context of the book as a whole, we readily see that it also shares the larger topic of the first narrative: the experiences of the non-native teacher. We also note how the second narrative seems to "fit into" or "make sense" within the first; using terminology discussed in more detail in Benson (2011), we might say that the second narrative recounts an "incident" in the larger language teaching and learning "career" that is recounted in the first narrative.

Medgyes is a skilled and articulate storyteller and in our experience many other teachers and learners have similar stories to tell about their experiences with the languages they teach and learn. These stories have three main characteristics that mark them off from other kinds of narratives. First, they are mainly narratives of personal experience, or as we described them earlier, autobiographical narratives. Second, they typically recount experiences of language teaching and learning as experiences that are set in the context of the teller's real or imagined everyday life. Third, they typically involve aspects of the narrators' identities. Indeed it may be through such narratives that individuals mark out language teaching and learning as significant areas of their lives and develop and manage their identities as language teachers or learners.

1.4 Narrative Inquiry in Language Teaching and Learning Research

The advice on narrative research methodology offered in this book is based on analysis of a database of more than 175 papers on language teaching and learning in which narrative plays an important part. These papers were drawn from several collections focused on narrative inquiry (Barkhuizen, 2011; Benson and Nunan, 2002, 2004; Casanave and Schechter, 1997; Johnson and Golombek, 2002; Kalaja, Barcelos and Menezes, 2008) and also include numerous journal articles and book chapters that have been published elsewhere over the last ten years or so. Although the number of narrative inquiry papers remains small in comparison to those that use more established approaches, it is sufficient for certain patterns to have emerged. Whereas methodological commentaries on narrative inquiry have hitherto drawn mainly on advice from sources beyond language teaching and learning research (Bell, 2002; Benson, 2004; Cameron, 2000; Kouritzin, 2000b; Oxford, 1995; Pavlenko, 2002, 2007), we are now able to supplement this advice with insights from research in our own field. In this section, we introduce some of the studies we draw on later in the book, grouping them into five broad categories according to the overall approach to narrative and narrative inquiry.

Language memoirs are informally written accounts of language learning experiences, often written for non-academic readers. Two of the best known book-length language memoirs are Eva Hoffman's (1989) *Lost in Translation* and Alice Kaplan's (1993) *French Lessons: A Memoir*. Memoirs are not usually considered as "research," although Kaplan (1994) explains that she decided to write her memoir out of a sense that academic writing did not really capture the reality of what it was like to learn a foreign language. Several collections of memoirs in which language researchers have written about their own language learning experiences straddle the boundary between personal and reflective writing and research (Belcher and Connor, 2001; Nunan and Choi, 2010; Ogulnick, 2000). There are also memoirs that focus more on teaching than on learning (Casanave and Schecter, 1997; Curtis and Romney, 2006; Johnson and Golombek, 2002; Vandrick, 2009). Described in terms of the distinctions introduced in the previous section, language memoirs are autobiographical, by definition, and involve narrative analysis (rather than analysis of narrative), because the work that goes into them mainly consists in the construction of the narratives. Whether or not language memoirs count as research is really a matter of convention, and largely depends on how far we are prepared to accept that recollections can constitute research data and that reflection and writing can constitute methods of data analysis.

Studies of language memoirs fall clearly into the domains of biography and analysis of narratives, because the researchers play no part in the writing of the narratives studied and usually apply non-narrative methods to their analysis. Authors typically take one or more published memoirs and analyze them thematically. Two very different examples of this kind of research are found in studies by Pavlenko (2001a, 2001b, 2001c), which analyze aspects of the language learning memoirs of immigrants to North America, and Takeuchi (2003), which systematically investigated the learning strategies mentioned in Japanese writers' memoirs of English language learning.

Autobiographical case studies of learners' and teachers' experiences are similar to memoirs in many ways, but differ in being written for academic readers and in involving both narrative analysis and analysis of narratives. Benson and Nunan's (2002) collection, which aimed to explore "the experience of language learning" through learners' stories, included several autobiographical studies, including He's (2002) and Sakui's (2002) narrative accounts of their lifelong experiences of learning and teaching English. Both papers include substantial sections in which the authors tell their stories, but He also includes an analysis of the different learning strategies that she used in China, Australia, and Hong Kong, while Sakui, who situates her paper in the field of "self-study" (Loughran and Russell, 2002), analyzed the influence of her learning experiences on her experience as a writing teacher. Diary studies, such as Campbell's (1996) study of her experience of studying abroad in Mexico are a particular form of autobiographical study, in which the data are collected concurrently with the experience investigated and later reviewed and analyzed. The fact that autobiographical studies typically involve additional analysis of the autobiographical narrative seems to make them more readily accepted as research studies.

Biographical case studies are studies of individuals, in which the researchers elicit data from the participant and write them up as narratives, possibly for further analysis. Tsui (2007) is an example of a biographical case study of an EFL teacher's career in China. The findings of the paper take the form of a narrative of the teacher's career, followed by an analysis of the data based on Wenger's (1998) theory of identity formation. It is also in studies of this kind that we are most likely to find co-construction of narratives and co-authorship with participants. So and Dominguez's (2004) study of emotion processes in language learning emerged from conversations between the first and second authors, which were recorded and formed the basis for the co-constructed narrative.

Studies of multiple narratives are similar to biographical case studies, with the main difference being the number of participants, which can vary from two to several hundred. Menard-Warwick (2004) is a comparison of two biographical case studies of female immigrant language learners, while Shedivy (2004) consists of five case studies of university-level students of Spanish. At the other end of the spectrum are language learning history studies such as Oxford's (2001) study of students' conceptions of teachers, in which the researcher analyzed metaphors in 473 short narratives. In these kinds of studies the narratives are usually written and the researchers play no role in their construction, other than giving the writers instructions on what they should write about. In some cases the narrative data remain available for other kinds of analysis by the same or other researchers. In this respect, studies of multiple narratives have much in common with studies of language memoirs (the main difference that the narratives are elicited rather than "found"). These two categories of narrative inquiry also differ from the other three in that they use narratives as data (analysis of narratives), but do not typically involve the construction of narratives by the researchers (narrative analysis).

These five categories account for most of the studies in our database, which are either based on narrative inquiry methodologies or contain substantive treatment of narratives. In Section 1.2 we introduced three distinctions within approaches to narrative inquiry: between (1) narrative analysis and analysis of narratives, (2) autobiographical and biographical approaches, and (3) focus on content and focus on language and discourse. Table 1.1 illustrates how the five categories differ

TABLE 1.1 Types of narrative inquiry in language teaching and learning research

	Narrative analysis	Analysis of narratives	Autobiography	Biography
Language memoirs	Yes	No	Yes	No
Studies of language memoirs	No	Yes	No	Yes
Autobiographical studies	Yes	Yes	Yes	No
Biographical case studies	Yes	Yes	No	Yes
Studies of multiple narratives	No	Yes	No	Yes

in terms of the first two distinctions. In relation to the third distinction, there is a strong focus on the content of narratives in all of the categories. As we mentioned earlier, studies that focus solely on the language and discourse of narratives fall outside the scope of this book, because they do not address issues of language teaching and learning. However, many of the studies that we will look at in this book do involve attention to the language and discourse of the narratives they analyze (for example, Oxford's 2001 study of metaphors). In this context, it is worth noting the emergence of a possible sixth category, consisting of studies using a "small story" approach to explore issues of second language teaching, learning, and use through analysis of narratives (Barkhuizen, 2010; Holmes and Marra, 2011; Rugen, 2010; Simpson, 2011). These could be included in the "biographical case studies" category, although an important feature of them is that the narratives are not elicited, but collected from naturally occurring conversations ("small stories" being short excerpts of these conversations). In the four studies cited, there is also a focus on the content of the narratives, but more important is the focus on the ways in which the participants use narratives in particular contexts of interaction, such as the classroom or the multilingual workplace.

In addition to the narrative inquiry studies that form the basis of this book, there are many other language teaching and learning studies in which narratives play a role. Baker and MacIntyre's (2000) study of non-linguistic outcomes of French immersion and non-immersion programs, for example, is mainly based on quantitative analysis of responses to questionnaire items, but the questionnaire also included an item that asked respondents to write a short narrative about a positive or negative experience of speaking French. Narrative plays similar complementary roles in other approaches with their own distinctive methodologies, including ethnography (Norton, 2000; McKay and Wong, 1996), longitudinal case studies (Schmidt, 1983; Teutsch-Dwyer, 2001), and stimulated recall interviews (Roebuck, 2000). Indeed, wherever the research approach involves development over time, narrative is likely to play a part, either in the nature of the data that is analyzed (open-ended questionnaire responses, interview transcripts, diaries, observation notes, and recall protocols often include narratives or take a narrative form) or in writing up the findings. None of the studies cited in this paragraph claim to use a narrative approach, yet when we read them with the idea of narrative inquiry in mind, we begin to see narrative at work in them at a number of levels.

This broader presence of narrative in language teaching and learning research reflects a broader turn towards qualitative methodologies in language teaching and learning research in recent years (Benson, et al., 2009; Heigham and Croker, 2009; Richards, 2003, 2009) that is inspired by sociocultural critiques of the reliance on "scientific" experimental and survey methods in the search for cognitive universals in Second Language Acquisition research (Benson, 2004; Block, 2003; Firth and Wagner, 1997; Lantolf and Pavlenko, 2001; Norton and Toohey, 2001). One of the most important elements in these critiques, which emphasize both the social and the individual (Benson and Cooker, 2013), is a more intensive focus on the people who actually teach and learn languages and how the activities of teaching and learning languages fit into their lives. As Lantolf and Pavlenko (2001: 145) put it, these new approaches treat language learners not as "processing devices," but as "people," who "actively engage in constructing the terms and conditions of their own learning"; or in Norton and Toohey's (2001: 310) words, they are concerned "not only with studying individuals acting on L2 input and producing L2 output, but also with studying how L2 learners are situated in specific social, historical, and cultural contexts." Although there is no necessary connection between sociocultural approaches to theory and qualitative or narrative approaches to research methodology, there is an affinity between them that arises from a shared interest in particularistic knowledge. Narrative inquiry can also be viewed as an especially apt approach to investigate how language teachers and learners are situated in specific social, historical, and cultural contexts, in which the primary context is viewed as the teachers' and learners' lives.

1.5 Topics in Narrative Inquiry

This book is mainly concerned with methodologies in narrative inquiry and how they can be applied in research on language teaching and learning. In principle, narrative inquiry can be applied to any topic within this field, although it would seem to be more valuable in some areas than in others. Much depends on the creativity of the researcher, however. Phonology, for example, would seem to be an unpromising field for narrative inquiry, yet Marx's (2002) study of accent and second language identity shows that this is far from being the case. What we might say, therefore, is that even in areas where other methodologies dominate, narrative inquiry can provide complementary perspectives. One of the sources for narrative inquiry in our field is the rich tradition of narrative studies of teachers' lives, in which there are numerous studies of second and foreign language teachers (Casanave and Schecter, 1997; Curtis and Romney, 2006; Johnson and Golombek, 2002). There have been far fewer narrative inquiry studies of learners and learning in the field of education, however, and it is perhaps in this area that language researchers have made a distinctive contribution. Topics within the area of language learning include learning strategies (He, 2002; Malcolm, 2004), motivation (Lim, 2002; Shoaib and Dörnyei, 2004), persistence (Cotterall, 2004; Sataporn and Lamb, 2004; Shedivy, 2004; Umino, 2004), affect (Aoki, 2002; Carter, 2002; Oxford, 1995; So and Dominguez, 2004), age (Bellingham, 2004), individual difference (Chik, 2007), autonomy and self-directed learning (Benson, Chik, and Lim, 2003; Murray, 2004; Murray and Kojima, 2007), and learning with technology (Chik and Breidbach, 2011a, 2011b). There have also been studies of second language literacy (Bell, 1997; Connor, 1999; Shen, 1989), bilingual parenting (Fries, 1998; Kouritzin, 2000a), language policy (Lam, 2002), experiences of emigration and transplantation (Block, 2002; Kanno, 2000, 2003; Kouritzin, 2000c; Pavlenko, 1998, 2001a, 2001b), and language loss (Hinton, 2001).

Within this research, we can also identify a number of emerging themes that appear to be especially characteristic of narrative inquiry in our field: identity, context, and affect. One point to make in relation to these themes is that the most distinctive quality of narrative inquiry is its capacity to provide access to long-term experiences through retrospection and imagination. Language teaching and learning careers can often occupy much of teachers' and learners' lives, and they develop both inside and outside classrooms and schools. Whatever its limitations may be, narrative inquiry is the only methodology that provides access to language teaching and learning as lived experiences that take place over long periods of time and in multiple settings and contexts. It is for this reason, perhaps, that identity has emerged as the single most frequently mentioned theme in narrative studies of teaching and learning. To some extent narrative inquiry in this area can be viewed as a matter of the investigation of the development of second language identities over time. Time becomes a crucial issue here, because, as Block (2002: 2) argues, "prolonged contact with an L2 and a new and different cultural setting causes irreversible destabilization of the individual's sense of self." Narrative research has also tended to show that it is through this prolonged contact that individuals develop identities as "learners" or "teachers" of second or foreign languages.

Context has emerged as an equally important theme, however, because, as Oxford (1996: 582) puts it, "when language learners are asked to tell their histories, they inevitably address contextual, situational, cultural factors as part of the story of their learning." Context is a pervasive theme in language teaching and learning research, but the distinctive feature of narrative inquiry is, perhaps, its capacity to address this theme through the context of learners' and teachers' life experiences and their own construal of what is contextually relevant to their learning or teaching. Affect, our third theme, arises from the ways in which autobiographical accounts tend to bring the emotional dimensions of language teaching and learning, which are often suppressed by other research approaches, to the fore. As Oxford (1996: 582) again puts it, "as reflections on situated cognition, language learning histories often evoke a wealth of emotions and other affective reactions from the language learner."

To conclude this introduction, we note an observation by Pavlenko (2002) on language memoirs, which is relevant to our earlier comment on the role of narrative inquiry in creating space for a greater diversity of voices in research. Pavlenko observes that "language learning memoirs provide a wealth of observations about learning experiences of middle-class Caucasian, Asian, and Latin American females, but observations about the role of gender in language learning of heterosexual males, homosexual learners, working-class individuals, or African immigrants are rather scarce" (p. 216). This comment was made a decade ago and does not take account of recent publications or the ways in which narrative research has moved beyond the publication and study of language memoirs. We are aware of publications that fall into the categories of absence that Pavlenko identifies. Nevertheless, it remains true that we hear more of some kinds of voices than we do of others in narrative inquiry (Cadman and Brown, 2011; Canagarajah, 1996). Narrative inquiry is, perhaps, most empowering when it involves autobiography, and from this perspective Curtis and Romney's (2006) collection of autobiographical studies focusing on issues of race and color in language teaching is one important contribution to the field. Another more recent collection is that of Nunan and Choi (2010) which presented stories of language learners that highlighted their understandings of culture and identity. What these collections illustrate is that the landscape of narrative inquiry in language teaching and learning is a shifting landscape that is capable of reshaping itself in response to new interests and concerns. Whatever we have to say about topics, themes, and participants today will be constantly subject to revision and we hope this book will encourage readers to make their own contribution to this developing field.

2
ORAL NARRATIVES

2.1 Introduction

In Chapters 2–4, we introduce different forms of narrative data, including oral narratives (Chapter 2), written narratives (Chapter 3), and multimodal narratives (Chapter 4). In narrative inquiry, interviews are mainly used to elicit oral accounts of language learning and teaching experiences. In this chapter, we look at the use of open and semi-structured interviews, and processing and transcription of oral accounts. The chapter first describes the kinds of narrative inquiry studies in which interviews are used (2.2). Second, featured studies that exemplify interview styles are discussed in some detail, and related research is also drawn on to present variations and extensions of interview techniques (2.3). In each case the data as well as the data-collection procedures are described. The chapter ends with a discussion of some of the challenges and ethical issues researchers face when working with oral narrative data (2.4).

2.2 Participants

In the published studies discussed in this chapter, interviews are conducted with a wide range of language learners and teachers and in different contexts, by researchers who frequently interview and transcribe themselves with or without the help of translators. Kvale and Brinkmann (2009: 102) divide interview inquiry into seven stages: thematizing, designing, interviewing, transcribing, analyzing, verifying, and reporting. Many narrative-based studies do not use interviewing as the only data collection method; interviews are frequently accompanied by other data collection methods. This section will give readers a better idea of the contexts in which interviews are conducted. These contexts included formal learning contexts (A), informal learning contexts with mature and heritage learners (B), informal contexts with migrant and sojourn learners (C), and formal contexts with pre- and in-service English teachers (D). Some of the studies that are referenced as examples are discussed in more detail later in the chapter.

A. Adult language learners recruited from formal learning contexts are interviewed to elicit their learning experiences (see Armour, 2001; Block, 1998; Cadman and Brown, 2011; Cotterall, 2004, 2008; and Sataporn and Lamb, 2004). In these studies, the interviewer-researchers do not necessarily teach the interviewees. In other studies interviews have been conducted as part of an action research project in which researchers wanted to have a better understanding of the courses or programs they were teaching or running (Block, 1996, 2002; Cotterall, 2008; Lo, 2009). There is a great variety of language learning contexts for such studies. For example, we have learners learning English in non-English-speaking countries (Benson and Gao, 2008; Chen, 2002; Chik, 2007, 2008, 2011; Gao, et al., 2002; Malcolm, 2004; Murray, 2008), learning French in French-speaking regions (Kinginger, 2004), learning Chinese in higher education (Lam, 2002), and learning Japanese in Japan (Casanave, 2012; Murray, 2004). The participants in these studies are usually adults who have a number of years of experience of language learning.

B. Mature learners and heritage language learners are interviewed to understand learning experiences beyond formal institutional contexts. Several narrative studies investigated the life-long language experiences among mature learners to explore the different roles of classroom and out-of-classroom experiences (Bellingham, 2004; Coffey and Street, 2008). Studies with mature learners usually allow researchers to retrospectively cover a longer period of language learning in different contexts and examine the role or impact of language learning at different life stages. Studies on heritage language learning among North American learners have also adopted a narrative approach (see for example, Coryell, et al., 2010, on Spanish; Lo, 2009, on Korean; and Shin, 2010, on a variety of heritage languages). These studies frequently make strong connections between one's identity and attitudes towards heritage languages, and language learning in both formal and informal learning environments.

C. Migrant and sojourn learner interviews constitute another strand of narrative interview research. The participants are often people who are adjusting to new living and/or learning environments. Interviews are conducted to capture their adjustment to new sociocultural, linguistic, and educational environments. Given that adjustments are required in both formal and personal contexts, learning is tied to various social worlds. These studies usually report the findings by creating strong and vivid narrative stories for the readers. Studies cover participants from various backgrounds, for example, South African immigrants in New Zealand (Barkhuizen, 2006; Barkhuizen and de Klerk, 2006), Taiwanese and Japanese students in the United Kingdom (Block, 2002), a Hong Kong student in the United Kingdom (Chik and Benson, 2008), new migrant mothers in Canada

(Kouritzin, 2000a, 2000c), Japanese youth in Canada (Kanno, 2000, 2003) and Chinese youth in the United States (McKay and Wong, 1996).

D. Pre-service and in-service English language teachers are interviewed to elicit their language teaching and/or learning experiences. In most cases, the interviewer-researchers are teaching or have taught postgraduate courses that the interviewees are taking or have taken. One research scenario is the provision of TESOL teacher education in English-speaking countries (see Case, 2004; Nam and Oxford, 1998; Reeves, 2009). Another common situation is the interviewing of non-native speakers of English language teachers in non-English-speaking countries (see Aoki with Hamakawa, 2003; Barkhuizen, 2010; Ellis, 2004; Hayes, 2010; Johnston, 1999; Liu and Xu, 2011; Reis, 2011; Tsui, 2007; Xu and Liu, 2009).

In narrative inquiry, it is not uncommon to adopt multiple methods of data collection, and interviewing is viewed as one technique among others (e.g., teacher journals, learner diaries, classroom observation). Coffey and Street (2008) explored the "figured worlds" of advanced foreign language learners by first asking the participants to write their language learning autobiographies, and then conducting semi-structured interviews. The spoken accounts contained spontaneous use of humor with stories from different life stages being told all at once, so they were chronologically less structured than the written accounts. Benson, et al. (2012, 2013) explored the development of second language identities of learners who opted for study abroad programs. The project adopted multiple methods of data collection: pre- and post-sojourn interviews, on-site interviews, blogging, and photograph elicitation. The study was also unusual in that it included participants from different age groups who studied overseas for different lengths of time.

2.3 Qualitative Research Interviewing for Narrative Inquiry

In the 1980s, van Lier (1988) stated that "few researchers ... have solicited learners' views of their language learning careers" (p. 79), but the contexts aforementioned suggest that the use of oral accounts of learning experiences has now become more popular in language teaching and learning research. Kvale and Brinkmann (2009) argue that "[t]he qualitative research interview attempts to understand the world from the subjects' points of view, to unfold the meaning of their experiences, to uncover their lived world prior to scientific explanations" (p. 1). Interviewing, thus, may be most suitable to be used for accessing personal perspectives on language learning and teaching in situated contexts. Kvale and Brinkmann (2009) identified three categories of interviews according to their purpose: short story, life story, and oral history. An interview that refers to a specific event is a short story. An interview that concerns a person's life story through his/her own retelling is a life history interview. And an oral history interview covers topics beyond the interviewee's personal history to communal history. In narrative inquiry, researchers quite frequently adopt a life history approach to capture long-term language learning experiences.

The format of interviews can be broadly categorized as a) structured, b) semi-structured, and c) open interviews (Kvale and Brinkmann, 2009; Mishler, 1986). The major distinction between the categories is the use of pre-set questions during the interview. In structured interviews, the researcher strictly follows the sequence of a set of prepared questions without wavering. Richards (2003: 69) views structured interviews as "oral questionnaires." One of the advantages of using structured interview is consistency. With pre-set questions and sequence, structured interviews may provide a more uniform collection of oral narratives in projects involving a larger number of participants. In discussing life history interviews, Atkinson (1998: 41) suggests that "*the less structure a life story interview has, the more effective it will be* in achieving the goal of getting the person's own story in the way, form, and style that the individual wants to tell it in" (p. 41, original emphasis).

The semi-structured interview is the most commonly used format in language teaching and learning research. Here the interviewer uses an interview guide with pre-set questions as "a resource that can be drawn on in whatever way and to whatever extent is appropriate" (Richards, 2003: 69). It is common that the interviewer has a set of core questions to anchor individual interviews, and to provide coherence across interviews. However, the use of semi-structured interviews also gives a certain degree of flexibility so that as the interview progresses the interviewer will ask follow-up questions for interviewees to clarify or elaborate. This provides an individual interview a distinctive "personality." Researchers have also used open interviews to elicit oral narratives. In an open interview, the interviewer does not use a set of interview questions. The interviewer may frame an open interview by stating his/her research interest and then let interviewees elaborate. We will discuss the two formats, semi-structured and open interview, in the following sections. For each referenced study, we also detail the steps taken by researchers to highlight different ways of designing and conducting interview studies.

2.3.1 Semi-structured Interviews

In semi-structured interviews, researchers use interview guides as resources to direct the interviews, but at the same time, the questions are usually open-ended to allow participants to elaborate and researchers to pursue developing themes. In addition to interview "guide," researchers have also used the term "protocol" or "schedule." An interview schedule is usually reserved for structured interviews. An interview protocol includes the interview questions and additional instructions to the interviewer or interviewees. In this chapter, we use the actual term used by the authors in the studies we review. Before setting the interview guide, Richards (2003) advises researchers to "decide on what the interview is setting out to achieve" and "identify the big questions" (p. 69). The interview questions should match the purpose of the interview. Coryell, et al. (2010) provided their interview questions in an appendix. Their study provides a good, transparent illustration of the connection between the questions and the oral narratives.

BOX 2.1

Coryell, Clark, and Pomerantz (2010) were interested in the reasons why bilingual heritage Spanish-English adult speakers in Texas wanted to take online Spanish courses at tertiary institutions. They wanted to know how these bilinguals' formal and informal experiences of Spanish learning influenced their current online learning. Their study aimed to provide a space for adult heritage language learners to discuss their lived experiences of learning Spanish in online settings. Data for the project consisted of face-to-face interviews and follow-up conversations with seven female learners. A thematic constant-comparison method was carried out to extract the narratives that highlighted the participants' reflections about Spanish in their online learning and home contexts. Drawing on Bormann's (1985) work on symbolic convergence theory, Coryell, et al. identified a "cultural fantasy metanarrative" of the acquisition of "proper" Spanish on the parts of the participants to construct their idealized bilingual identities. The narratives show that all participants wanted to learn "*True Spanish*" from formal language courses. This form of Spanish is different from the everyday conversational Spanish that most of the participants were already able to speak with varying levels of fluency. Participants related a true Spanish identity to the speaking of proper Spanish without using the local Tex-Mex variety. However, Coryell and her colleagues believe this form of "*True Spanish*" is only a cultural fantasy.

Coryell, et al. (2010) recruited seven female adult Spanish learners from two tertiary institutions in Texas. The study was conducted following these steps:

1. A call for participants was posted at two Texan institutions;
2. Seven female adult Spanish learners responded;
3. An initial semi-structured interview was conducted either through a face-to-face meeting in a community center office or via phone, and each interview lasted between one and a half and two hours;
4. An interview protocol was used;
5. All participants chose to be interviewed in English, with occasional use of Spanish for clarification or illustration;

6. Multiple follow-up conversations with each participant via email and/or telephone correspondence were conducted;
7. During the transcription process, each participant was contacted once for clarifications and supplementary explanation;
8. A total of thirteen hours of interview recordings and seventeen additional follow-up telephone and email discussions formed the core data set.

The interview questions Coryell and her colleagues used were well-structured for use in a language learning history (LLH) interview.

1. Which language do you consider your native or first language? Why?
2. In what other languages do you consider yourself fluent?
3. Do you consider yourself a good language learner?
4. Why did you decide to take this class online?
5. How do you feel about using computers and technology in your learning?
6. How do you know you are learning in your online course?
7. What kinds of online learning activities do you like best? Worst? Why?
8. How do you describe your own ethnicity or culture?
9. Tell me about your experience in learning languages other than English.
10. Tell me about online language learning experiences you have liked.
11. Tell me about experiences that may have been uncomfortable or disturbing with regard to your learning or practice in Spanish classes online.
12. How do you feel when you need to speak Spanish? (examples)
13. How do you feel using Spanish while native Spanish speaking people are present or when bilingual Americans learning Spanish are present? Why? How is the experience different? Can you give me some examples?
14. How do you feel writing in Spanish? (examples)
15. Do you think learning online is better or worse for learning a new language? Why?
16. How do you feel now after addressing this issue? (Coryell, et al., 2010: 469).

The interviewers used the above questions to focus the interview from the more general background questions (e.g., Question 1 to 3) to the project specific questions about online language learning (Question 4 to 11), and finally to specific issues related to Spanish learning and use (Question 12 to 16). The gradual progress also prepares interviewees to move from the more general to the more personal questions. The publication of the interview protocol gives readers a better sense of the ways the data were collected. It also provides a clear exemplar for researchers who are interested in either researching heritage language or using semi-structured interviews as a research tool. In the study, excerpts from interviews were presented to support the argument. For instance, when a participant stated she liked to use "real" Spanish, the following quotation was used to support the point:

I needed to get back into the proper, you know, language, and . . . not so much the enunciation, the enunciations you know are, are, pretty much the same in, in when you compare what's called Tex-Mex to proper Spanish. But, a lot of words are used incorrectly in Tex-Mex, and I wanted to get back to knowing exactly how to use the proper Spanish words that I was not using, that I knew I was not using right. (Coryell, et al., 2010: 462)

The number of questions in an interview guide may vary considerably, and the language used is usually everyday language (Kvale, 1996). When researchers reprint their interview schedules, it helps readers to make a stronger connection between the data collection process and the data presentation. It is especially helpful to see the various styles and forms of questions in interview schedules. In a study on learner identities, Block (2002) used six questions, but introduced academic linkage between language and identity and culture in his questions ("Many researchers now see language as inextricably tied up with identity and culture. What do you think of this idea? How has this link occurred in your experiences?"). Though the use of academic terms might have encouraged interviewees to answer the question in a particular way, the researcher was also making a more explicit statement about the purposes of the interviews. Bellingham (2004) included seven interview questions that she used with mature migrants in New Zealand to explore their perspectives on the ways older learners learn a new foreign language. In addition to general questions on background and specific questions on age-related language learning experiences, Bellingham asked "What advice would you give to a person over 40 starting to learn a new language?" at the end of her interviews (2004: 59). This last question is a good member-checking question because it allowed the researcher to cross-reference the narratives given earlier during the interviews. It also gave the interviewer space to confirm his interpretation with the interviewees. In a study with two early career English teachers, Reeves (2009) adopted a multi-method approach that included the collection of language learning biographies, casual conversation, classroom observation, and semi-structured interviews. In the interview guide, Reeves included an excellent question at the end to give interviewees the option of ending the interview or to elaborate further ("Do you have any other comments on your journey to becoming an ESL teacher?").

The studies discussed so far involved the use of one-to-one interviews. However, the use of focus group and group interviews is not uncommon, particularly in studies which employ multiple methods of data collection. A focus group usually has six to ten participants and a moderator. The format is usually non-directive, which means the moderator introduces a topic and then lets the participants express their opinions (Kvale and Brinkmann, 2009). Adopting a multiple case study approach, Rajadurai (2010) used focus group discussions to encourage interaction among participants to explore the use of English in out-of-class contexts among the Malaysian learners. Focus groups are a more interactive and dialogic data collection approach. Rajadurai argues that the situated interaction in a focus group, and the subsequent discourses that are produced, creates a "community narrative" (p. 97) to validate individual data collected through journal writing.

2.3.2 Open Interview

Richards (2003: 65) views interviewing not as getting an "answer" to a particular question, but as "a journey within a journey." The use of open interviews best exemplifies this. With open interviews, or unstructured interviews, the interviewer sets up the interview with no specified pre-set questions or agenda (Connelly and Clandinin, 1990). However, Jones (1985, cited in Richards, 2003) does not believe that open or non-directive interviews really exist because the interviewees will be speculating about the intention and agenda of the interviewers. In advising on life story interviews in the field of sociology, Chase (2003) suggests that researchers should formulate questions that invite the interviewees to tell their stories in their own words, phrase questions in everyday language, and should not orient the interviewees towards the researchers' interest. During the interview, Chase recommends, "reiterating the invitation [to tell a story] through questions that encourage fuller narration of the complexities of [the interviewee's] story" (p. 289). Richards (2011) suggests that the interviewer should be sensitive to their use of minimal responses (e.g., *yeah, uh-huh,* etc.) during the interview, as these seemingly benign responses may indicate the interviewer's position.

Although open interviews are not adopted very frequently in narrative inquiry, Gao, et al. (2002) used them to "provide ample freedom for the informants to narrate their language-learning stories, explore events and themes that they deemed critical or important for self-identity development" (p.98). In open interviews, researchers usually provide a general framework for the interviewees, and then encourage them to direct the interviews. Gao, et al. (2002) used one elicitation question in the beginning: "I'd be interested to know why you learn English, and what changes—feelings, ideas, understanding of yourself, etc.—you have experienced in your learning. Can you walk me through the process, from your middle school time to the present?" (p. 99). While Gao, et al. (2002) used one elicitation question, in a study with an Arab learner (Hamad), Malcolm (2004) gave the learner a set of questions to consider before their first meeting. Malcolm and the participant met four times over two weeks. During the interviews, Hamad "began to talk about his college English courses, and he frequently sidetracked and returned to it when talking about what seemed to be unrelated matters, such as how his listening improved when he took a course at a private institute" (p. 82). This postscript shows that in open interviews, though the participant may be aware of the overall agenda and direction, diversion is inevitable. Cotterall (2004) used open interviews and a longitudinal design to explore one learner's negotiation of his learning agenda.

BOX 2.2

> Cotterall (2004) aimed to explore a learner's goals and beliefs about language learning during a beginner's language course. She was particularly interested in the amount of control the learner had over his learning process. The study adopted a longitudinal approach and Cotterall held six interviews over a four-month period. Open interviews were used with the participant, and he was encouraged to elaborate on any topics or issues that were important to him. The interview data revealed three key themes: "the gradual narrowing of the learner's goals, the learner's fluctuating affective state and his changing conceptualizations of the nature of language learning" (p.107). Cotterall shows that an open dialogue with a learner can highlight the emotional undercurrents in a learner's experience of his language course over a semester, and how these emotions accounted for his changing views and ultimate disappointment with the Spanish introductory course.

Cotterall (2004) treated the interactive interviews with her research "partner," Harry, as "co-constructed discourse events" (Block, 2000: 759). It is unusual in this study that the term "partner" is used instead of a "participant." It signals the co-constructed nature of this particular study (see also the discussion of "participant" in Chapter 1).

1. Harry was recruited in the second week of the Spanish class;
2. Harry and Cotterall met in her office every two weeks from March to June, 1999;
3. Six interview sessions were conducted, and each session lasted for about an hour;
4. Cotterall started each session with open-ended questions, but these questions were not reported;
5. The interviews were audio-recorded and transcribed;
6. The interview data were treated as "a product of the interaction between interviewer and interviewee" (Block, 2000: 759);
7. The transcript was sent to Harry for his comments;
8. The draft chapter (Cotterall, 2004) was sent to Harry for his comments.

These procedures provide readers with some guidance on planning an open-interview study. Cotterall cited the rapport built between her and Harry, and also his own confidence and open nature, as the keys to the study. In the spirit of co-construction, Cotterall tried to retain as much of Harry's own words as possible. As a result, the excerpts presented in the chapter retained some features of spoken discourse, for instance, when Harry first discussed his previous experience at university:

> I mucked around at Otago University a couple of y- about s- five or six seven years ago achieved very little arrived there with a hangover and . . . ended up just having a lot of fun and going to heaps of parties and . . . virtually did nothing. (Cotterall, 2004: 107)

Throughout the study, Cotterall constantly sought Harry's comments and feedback on her interpretation of the interviews, which was important in building a supportive environment for the open interviews. Harry felt so comfortable that he was happy to make the following statement:

> as an interviewer . . . you made me feel absolutely comfortable. Apart from anything else, you became the person upon whom I unloaded my anxieties, and with whom I shared my triumphs, re my Spanish. In that light then, it is easy to understand why things seemed to flow with great fluidity. (Cotterall, 2004: 106)

In using open interview, as suggested by Cotterall, the interaction between the researcher and the participant is the main driving force in shaping the direction of the interview. In such studies, researchers tend to use "conversation" in place of "interview" to signal the informal and dialogical nature of the event. So and Domínguez's (2004) study involved six conversations between So and Domínguez, and the LLH written by Domínguez:

> Rocío [Domínguez] agreed to meet with me [So] regularly for the next couple of months, simply recounting her recent experience related to her acquisition of the English language. I remained a listener, occasionally asking questions for clarification and further detail. We met six times in total for this purpose for about an hour each time between 28 October 1998 and 8 February 1999. Like the day of our first session, the day for the last session had not been pre-planned. When we both felt we had seen sufficient number of 'interesting' things in Rocío's stories, we were eager to switch our dialogist hat to that of the researcher. (p. 42)

The conversation was later transcribed verbatim by Domínguez and she also wrote "a narrative of her background and previous language-related experiences" (p. 54) for the project. The study generated a strong partnership during the data collection and analysis, and Domínguez was credited as the second author.

2.3.3 Frequency and Length of Data Collection

In published studies, the duration of interviews varies greatly from half an hour to several hours per session. Though the usual length, as reported by researchers, is under one and a half hours, Tsui (2007) reported using four "intensive face-to-face conversations" of about four hours each over the period of one week (p. 659). It was an extraordinary situation as Tsui met her participant during a conference, which explained the number of interviews conducted during a short period of time. Richards (2003) advises that the duration of each interview should be viewed in light of the constraints and opportunities provided by the interviewees. He also suggested that both interviewer and interviewee may experience tiredness after an hour of interviewing, and this can affect the quality of the interview.

Other than deciding on duration of the interview, the length of learning history covered by an interview should also be considered. Some studies have covered whole LLHs (see Chik, 2007; Coffey and Street, 2008), but most cover shorter periods of time, from a few weeks to several months. One common feature of conducting interviews in narrative inquiry is sequencing interviews over a period of time. The choice of sequencing and arrangement of interviews will affect one dimension of the interview: retrospective or concurrent interviewing. In retrospective interviewing, participants only discuss past language learning experiences. In this type of interviewing, researchers are interested in how past events might have shaped certain present practices (e.g., preferences in language learning strategies). In concurrent interviewing, participants discuss both their past and current language learning experiences. In concurrent interviewing, participants may very well be taking language courses in formal contexts or adjusting to new linguistic environments. Participants then recount their past history of language learning, as well as learning experiences and incidents that take place during the period of data collection. Cotterall (2004) scheduled six interview sessions with her participant, Harry, to elicit his prior LLH and his experiences of taking the Spanish class during the period of study. Swain and Miccoli (1994) conducted seven interviews over a two-month period with their participant in order to explore the emotive and social aspects of learning English as a second language in a small group setting. The first interview was framed as a get-to-know-each-other type of interview to gain retrospective accounts of language learning. Subsequent interviews were based on observation of the participant in the classroom and field notes by the researchers. The participant also wrote notes on the process of language learning, which were then turned into stimuli for two interviews (the third and fourth). An additional eighth interview was conducted to gain consensus and comments from the participant on the transcripts of the interviews and preliminary data analysis. Swain and Miccoli (1994) is a good example of scheduling concurrent interviews to gain both retrospective accounts and learning experience during a course.

The length of time over which data is collected varies dramatically in published studies. Study abroad case studies by Kinginger (2004) and Chik and Benson (2008) both reported a data collection period of about four years. Other studies cited time frames from a shorter period of one to two weeks (Armour, 2001; Block, 1998; Ellis, 2004; Lam, 2002; Malcolm, 2004; Tsui, 2007) to several months (Armour, 2004; Barkhuizen, 2010; Cotterall, 2004; Swain and Miccoli, 1994) to years (Kanno, 2000; Reeves, 2009). However, it should be noted that though some studies indicate a shorter period of oral interview data collection, the interview data is supplemented by a longer period of classroom observation or artifact examination. The unusually long period of data collection in Chik and Benson (2008) is justified by the nature of the study: the natural length of study abroad for an undergraduate degree.

BOX 2.3

Chik and Benson (2008) followed the undergraduate study of one Hong Kong student, Ally, in Manchester, United Kingdom. They were interested in "understanding the experience of study overseas from the student's perspective and within the context of the student's life" (p. 156). Rather than conceiving bilinguals as members of multiple language communities with the L1 and L2 worlds existing side by side (Kanno, 2000), Chik and Benson use the term "frequent flyer" to signal the back and forth character of their experience. Their data included three unstructured interviews that spanned over four years, with each interview scheduled at a critical point of Ally's overseas study: pre-departure, midway, and after Ally returned to Hong Kong.

Because Chik and Benson (2008) set out to investigate the different learning experience during a student's overseas study, they took the following steps:

1. The interviewer (Chik) met with Ally before she left for Manchester, UK, in 2003;
2. The second interview was held two years (2005) later when Ally was on her summer break in Hong Kong;
3. The final interview was held about six months after Ally completed her degree and returned to Hong Kong in 2007;
4. The three interviews were unstructured and each lasted around 90 to 120 minutes;
5. The interviews were conducted in a mixture of Cantonese and English.

This is one of the few studies that we know of that adopted a longitudinal approach in data collection. The long data collection period may not be practical or feasible or even necessary for researchers who are interested only in retrospective data. A study abroad project by Benson, et al. (2012, 2013) also adopted a longitudinal approach to explore the development of second language identities among sojourn learners from different age groups. In studies that explore changes and developments in learners, a longitudinal approach will certainly yield rich data.

2.3.4 Data Transcription

Transcription is the process of turning recorded speech into written form. Kvale and Brinkmann (2009) view transcriptions as "translations from an oral language to a written language" (p. 178). There are no fixed rules for transcription, and the format of transcription is often a choice made by individual researchers based on the intended use of the transcripts. However, if there is more than one transcriber, Kvale and Brinkmann (2009) recommend stating explicitly how transcriptions are done for transparency and consistency. Though Lapadat (2000) demonstrates, with reference to empirical work, that transcription may vary according to research aims and needs, it is not common to see the inclusion of transcription conventions in published narrative work. Kinginger's (2004) study of an American learner of French is one exception, with the inclusion of the transcription conventions in the appendix.

Transcribing verbatim, which means word-for-word transcription that includes the non-verbal elements in interviewer-interviewee interaction, is a common way of handling oral data. Verbatim transcripts frequently give a feeling of rawness with non-standard grammatical utterances, repetition, or informal phrases as they naturally occur in spoken interaction. Kvale (1996) cautions that the publication of verbatim transcripts may project unfavorable images of the participants. Bellingham (2004) and Malcolm (2004) both used verbatim transcription because these researchers were interested in the content of the interviews; they were not edited for grammatical accuracy. Rajadurai (2010) used focus group interviews, and the data were orthographically transcribed, which meant the interactions were transcribed as spoken but minus any grammatical errors. The excerpts presented in Coryell, et al. (2010) show features of spoken discourse (e.g., expression and hesitation).

Most interview-based studies cited in this chapter did not use detailed transcription. However, the recent interest in "small stories" (Bamberg, 1997) has highlighted the value of detailed transcriptions for "positioning analysis" of interaction within interviews. Barkhuizen (2010) was interested in the imagined "better life" of a migrant pre-service teacher, and he included a detailed transcription of a segment of his second interview for in-depth analysis. The 114-line transcript printed as an appendix to the paper provided clarity to the analytical process. A similar transcription was used in Simpson's (2011) study of how EFL students used discursive space to connect learning and their personal lives. Simpson's study also included intonation and other conventions to indicate speech features like overlapping and inaudible components. The studies by Barkhuizen (2010) and Simpson (2011) show that the transcription process should match the analytical intent.

In narrative inquiry, researchers are interested in aspects of second and foreign language learning, and thus the interviewees are usually bilingual or multilingual speakers who are learning a second or foreign language. Many interviews are conducted in English with interviewees who are second or foreign language learners. Pavlenko (2007) problematizes the use of one language (presumably English) with multilingual interviewees. She cites narrative studies in which people express themselves differently in different languages. In addition, interviewees may also position themselves differently with interviewers speaking languages other than English. However, Nekvapil (2003) showed that interviewing language doesn't make a difference. In many studies, the interviewers share the same linguistic backgrounds with the interviewees, thus allowing the possibility of bilingual interviewing. When interviewing bilingual or multilingual interviewees, researchers usually start by asking interviewees what their preference is regarding the language of the interview. For instance, Coryell, et al. (2010) indicated that their English-Spanish bilingual participants "each chose to communicate in the one-to-one interviews primarily in English, although they periodically used Spanish to clarify their examples and illustrate certain points" (p. 457). In a study on learner self-identity construction among Chinese learners (Gao, et al., 2002) the three participants chose to be interviewed in Chinese. The interviews were recorded and transcribed, and then the transcripts were coded. Extracts were translated into English to be included in the final manuscript. The English translations were "the informants' exact words, with some shortening and omission at the discourse level to avoid redundancy" (p. 99). Pavlenko (2007) recommends that transcript excerpts should be presented in both the original language and in translation to allow readers to make their own interpretation, and that two or more independent transcribers should conduct the translation. This advice may provide a higher level of coherence and accuracy in translation, but it may not be practical for researchers working on small-scale studies.

Studies that have used languages other than English as the interviewing language include: Japanese, in Aoki with Hamakawa (2003) and Umino (2004); Spanish, in Menard-Warwick (2004); and Chinese, in Chik (2007, 2008, 2011), Chik and Benson (2008), Gao, et al. (2002), Lam (2002), McKay and Wong (1996), Miller (2011), and Xu and Liu (2009). In bilingual or multilingual interviews, it is common for researchers to present English versions of foreign language narratives. In most of the studies cited here, the researchers are frequently the translators as well. In interviews with bi- or multilingual interviewees, it is not uncommon for the interviewees to code-mix or code-switch. Although transcription depends on the aims and purposes of the study, Lapadat (2000) suggests that researchers should also incorporate the exact phrases of code-mixing. In Chik (2008), the interviewees primarily used Cantonese during the interviews; phrases in English are indicated in the excerpts. When an American-Chinese returnee student discussed his English learning in Hong Kong, he stated:

> I put in a lot of efforts . . . {In the areas of writing and grammar}, the use of vocabulary, organization, and speech writing. I learnt all these in Hong Kong. (Chik, 2008: 26)

The phrase in brackets indicates the participant's use of English in an otherwise Cantonese interview. English-Afrikaans participants in Barkhuizen and de Klerk (2006) on migrant language experience in South Africa and New Zealand chose to be interviewed in English, but frequently code-switched to Afrikaans. In the excerpts, Barkhuizen and de Klerk provided the excerpts in English with the Afrikaans phrases in the original format. The English translation was provided in brackets. In the following example, an interviewee described his imagined in adaptation to learning English in New Zealand:

> I'm gonna struggle in the beginning because I'm Afrikaans, it's my first language, but *ek sal moet aanpas* [I will have to adapt]. I know, I have to. But it is not a concern for me. I am easy, *ek sal maklik aanpas, nie gemaklik aanpas nie, maar ek gaan nie daarteen skree nie. Ek weet ek moet dit doen* [I will adapt easily, not comfortably, but I won't shout against it. I know I must do it]. (Barkhuizen and de Klerk, 2006: 286)

In addition to providing the interview excerpts in both original language and English, researchers can provide clear descriptions of the steps involved in the translation and transcription process. Xu and Liu (2009) is a good example.

BOX 2.4

Xu and Liu (2009) were explicit about their process of interviewing and transcribing. In a study exploring teachers' experiences with assessment reform in China, Xu and Liu conducted two three-hour semi-structured interviews with a teacher participant in Chinese. The choice of interview language was justified by allowing the participant to better express herself. The interview data were first transcribed verbatim in Chinese before being translated into English. To strengthen the reliability of the translated versions, Xu and Liu asked two other Chinese-speaking EFL colleagues to read the translation to check for accuracy. They then condensed the Chinese interview transcripts and transformed them, using English, into three narratives about assessment practices. The final narratives were also crosschecked with the original Chinese transcripts. In their final presentation of the narratives, only the English versions were presented.

Though the stages of turning oral data into written data may be a common practice, it is helpful to readers when these steps are stated explicitly in the published report. Xu and Liu (2009) showed clearly how oral data were transcribed, translated, and used in their study.

2.4 Problems and Ethical Issues

As in other types of research, there are some basic ethical guidelines for narrative researchers to follow. First, participants should be fully informed of the purposes of the project. Second, researchers should obtain the participants' informed consent to participate in the study. The informed consent should be written in plain language, and should provide detailed information about the use of data collected for the project. Third, researchers should also be sensitive to changes in participants' lives. For instance, new family, academic or work commitments may prompt withdrawal from the project. Finally, participants should be promised full confidentiality, and researchers should work to ensure that the transcript is loyal to the participants' oral statements.

In studies related to second and/or foreign languages, issues of language in interviewing can also be tricky. Though Pavlenko (2007) advocates multilingual interviewing with multilingual speakers, she also acknowledges the challenges of exhaustion and availability. Many interviewees in published narrative inquiry studies are learners of English with various levels of proficiency, and they were interviewed in English. The issue of language choice is perhaps best illustrated in Miller's (2011) study with a Chinese Cantonese-speaking immigrant. Miller and her Cantonese undergraduate student assistant conducted three semi-structured interviews with the participant: twice in English and once in Cantonese. Readers were provided with the transcripts of all three interviews, and the interview conducted in Cantonese was noticeably richer. The English transcript of the Cantonese interview shows that the interviewee spoke in much longer turns with fuller explanations of his own position as a non-native English speaker in the work environment. The Cantonese interview was transcribed and translated by an undergraduate student, and though Miller mentioned potential methodological issues which could arise when using an interpreter, she claimed that the additional information provided in the Cantonese interview enabled the interviewee's agency.

Kouritzin (2000c) explored immigrant mothers' thoughts about learning English, their family's experiences of immigration and settlement, and their children's education in Canada. She used a life-history interview approach and the interviews were conducted in English. Kouritzin defended her decision to ask participants with lower levels of proficiency in English to be interviewed in English based on her own experiences of speaking Japanese in Japan:

> I was filled with resentment when people resorted to translators because they assumed that I couldn't make myself understood. The message I got was that they didn't want to spend the time or energy it would take for us to converse in Japanese . . . I think the use of interpreters negates the feeling of pride that second language speakers often have when they discover for themselves that they can make themselves understood in a foreign language. (2000c: 18)

Kouritzin (2000c) also viewed the use of translators as not particularly helpful for building rapport between interviewer and interviewee. Based on our own research experience, we believe it is important for researchers to allow interviewees to choose the interview language, especially if they share the same linguistic backgrounds.

In addition to the interview language, the selection of the venue for conducting interviews needs to be carefully made. During interviews, participants may share some very personal experiences, and they would therefore appreciate some privacy. In a study on non-native English teachers' adjustment, Case (2004) stated that to ensure confidentiality, the venue for the interviews was clear of students and colleagues. The venue should be quiet enough to provide an environment conducive to conversation. Some participants, however, may prefer public places (e.g., a café or community center) to work or school settings. Participants should be consulted about their preferences when arranging interviews. To provide a general guide to our readers, the following checklist can be used as a helpful reminder when conducting semi-structured interviews.

BOX 2.5

Checklist for conducting semi-structured interview

Pre-interview

1. Prepare in writing an interview guide with more general biographical questions to start and then proceed to questions relevant to the research agenda;

- the questions should be open-ended enough for the interviewee to respond freely;
- the questions should be phrased in everyday language (not academic jargon).

2. Design a consent form that includes the permission to use interview excerpts for research purposes, including academic publications.
3. Prepare the recording equipment:

   - the equipment should have new batteries or be fully charged;
   - check memory space for digital recording;
   - bring extra batteries or a charger;
   - ideally there should be two sets of recorders to safeguard good recording.

4. Choose a quiet and neutral venue for recording;

   - a café is appropriate for a more relaxing environment (but do not sit near the coffee making machine!);
   - alternatively, let the interviewee choose a comfortable and convenient location.

5. Confirm the interview date and time with the interviewee before the scheduled interview.
6. Do pay for the coffee and/or cake if you are conducting the interview at a café.

During the interview

7. Explain the interview agenda to the interviewee;
8. Let the interviewee read the consent form;
9. Ask for permission to record the interview;
10. Introduce the interview guide; or let the interviewee read the interview guide;
11. Turn on the recording equipment;
12. Draw on the interview guide but let the interviewee speak freely;
13. Take notes and ask for clarification and elaboration;
14. Let the interviewee find the natural close to the interview;
15. Offer the interviewee a copy of the recording.

Post-interview

16. Data management:

    - download and store the interview recording;
    - duplicate files for safe keeping.

17. Send the interviewee an appreciation card or email. This may be considered old-fashioned, but most participants appreciate the gesture;
18. Prepare an interview transcript;
19. Tidy up the interview transcript (it is not necessarily a good idea to show a verbatim transcript to the interviewee);
20. If necessary, send follow-up questions to the interviewee;
21. Share the transcript with the interviewee.

2.5 Conclusion

This chapter has presented four examples of studies based on oral narrative data. The first part of the chapter outlined various contexts in which such narratives are produced or elicited for the purposes of inquiry. The four featured studies illustrated variations in approaches to interviewing for oral narratives, and also highlighted issues relevant to data collection and handling. We concluded the chapter with a brief discussion of some of the ethical issues specifically related to the elicitation and handling of oral narrative data, and provided a checklist for conducting interviews. In Chapter 3, we will discuss different methods of eliciting written narratives.

3
WRITTEN NARRATIVES

3.1 Introduction

Written narrative data produced by language teachers and learners take many different forms. In this chapter we look at a range of these, including diaries, language learning histories (LLHs), reflective teacher journals, and narrative frames. The first part of the chapter describes the various contexts in which such narratives are written for the purposes of inquiry. Featured studies which exemplify the narrative data types constructed in different contexts are discussed in some detail, and related research is also drawn on to present variations and extensions of these data. In each case the data, as well as the data-collection procedures, are described. The chapter ends with a discussion of some of the challenges and ethical issues researchers face when working with written narrative data.

3.2 Contexts in which Written Narratives are Constructed

In language teaching and learning research, the different forms of written narrative data are constructed in a wide range of contexts, from language classrooms, to professional development programs, to the broader community beyond formal learning and teaching situations. In this chapter we focus on autobiographical studies, biographical case studies, and studies of multiple narratives.

To help readers orientate their own ideas for narrative inquiries, we outline here in more detail the contexts in which such data are written. Some of the studies that have been referenced as examples are discussed in more detail later in the chapter.

A. Language *learners* write about their *learning* experiences as participants in a research project, and the learners themselves are the researchers. They construct the written text, analyze it, and publish the findings. This work is thus clearly autobiographical. A typical example of written data produced in these contexts is learner diaries (e.g., Campbell, 1996).

B. Language *learners* write about their *learning* experiences as participants in a research project, but in this case, they are not the (primary) researchers. These biographical accounts of their learning are often the product of a course activity or assignment, which are then analyzed by the researcher (usually the instructor) for research purposes. The biographies can take the form of language learning histories (e.g., Murphey, Chen, and Chen, 2004; Barcelos, 2008; Oxford, 1995; Tse, 2000), journals, emails, and letters (Kinginger, 2004), and narrative frames (Macalister, 2012).

C. Pre-service and in-service language *teachers*, usually as part of coursework requirements, write about their language *learning* experiences in the form of learning diaries and journals (e.g., Oxford, 1995). Again, it is their instructors or other researchers who make use of the teachers' written data for analysis and publication.

D. Teachers and teacher educators write about their practice for professional development (as teachers or researchers). These studies use (auto)biographical data generated by the researchers for their own research purposes (Barkhuizen and Hacker, 2008; Sakui, 2002).

E. Language *teachers* (pre-service and in-service) write about their *teaching* practice for professional development, usually for a course activity or assignment. The goal of the writing is explicitly for the professional development of the teacher writers, and may take the form of reflective journals or stories (Barkhuizen, 2008a; Golombek and Johnson, 2004). They write about their own teaching experiences (past or present) and typically relate these to the content of the course that they are taking. However, the outcome of their reflections are used by researchers (again, usually their instructors) for further analysis as part of independent research projects.

F. Language *teachers* (pre-service and in-service) write about their *teaching* for a researcher. At the time of writing, teachers may or may not be participating in formal professional development courses, but even if they are the writing they produce is not specifically for their own professional development (although they may benefit from doing the writing). Rather, it is solicited by a researcher for their research purposes. The writing, usually in combination with other forms of data (typically interviews), can take the form of diaries (e.g., Tsui, 2007), reflective reports and journals (e.g., Liu and Xu, 2011; Poon, 2008), and narrative frames (Barkhuizen and Wette, 2008; Barnard and Nguyen, 2010; Wette and Barkhuizen, 2009).

The sections that follow present examples of studies that cover these possibilities. We begin by focusing on written data generated by language learners (diaries and learning histories), then examine teacher narratives (journals and other reflective writing), and finally we consider the use, benefits, and limitations of narrative frames for collecting data from both learners and teachers.

3.2.1 Learner Diaries

Learner diaries are autobiographical, introspective documents that record the experiences of language learning from the learner's perspective. Very much like personal diaries, they consist of a series of entries written over an extended period of time. Sometimes diaries record *general* reflections and observations, such as the writer's thoughts and feelings about their learning and stories of language-related successes and failures. If the writer's learning is classroom based, they may also comment on teaching, their teachers, and classroom activity. Diaries may have a more *specific* focus too, such as writing about learning strategies and styles, learner emotions, or cross-cultural encounters.

Benson (2004) points out that an important characteristic of learner diaries as narrative data is that they are written concurrently with the learning (written daily, for example, after classroom learning experiences, and in this respect they are retrospective). This means that diary studies are useful for researchers who aim to explore and understand affective factors, learning strategies, and the learners' own perceptions of their language learning through information that is recorded while learners are actually engaged in the process of learning. Diary studies make accessible data unobservable by other methods (Faerch and Kasper, 1987) providing a rich, full picture of learning, particularly the social and cognitive dimensions of learners from their particular point of view (Bailey, 1990). Campbell's (1996) study is a good example.

BOX 3.1

Campbell (1996) kept a diary during a two month visit to Mexico, where she planned to learn Spanish. Her aim was to explore how her prior language learning experience during a visit to Germany determined how she went about learning a new language. Although she was enrolled in a course, she felt the classes did not provide sufficient opportunities to communicate in Spanish and so she actively sought these outside the formal instructional setting, just like she did in Germany. Her strategy was to become friends with the teachers (she herself had teaching experience in the US) and to socialize with them in bars, restaurants, and at family gatherings. Campbell analyzed her diary for major themes related to this strategy and then compared her findings with other published language learning diary studies. The main finding of her study, in sum, was that she progressed in her acquisition of Spanish "by using the language in meaningful and psychological/emotionally charged situations" (p.214). Her learning strategy and the success she achieved thus reflected her prior language learning experience in Germany.

The following describes how Campbell went about constructing her narrative data:

1. Before leaving for Mexico she wrote a history of her previous language learning, and included this in her diary.
2. She wrote a daily journal, usually writing twice a day, early morning and afternoon.
3. Campbell skipped days occasionally but on the whole wrote regularly.
4. Each entry was about three or four handwritten notebook pages long.
5. On weekends she wrote more frequently and the entries were longer.
6. One entry was voice-recorded because so much had happened and she did not have time to write it all down. This was transcribed and included in the diary.
7. The diary contained seventy-one separate entries.
8. Five letters to friends back in the US were also included.

These procedures give some guidance for readers wishing to plan their own diary study. Important to note is that the project included some pre-writing which was incorporated into the diary. The writing was done regularly, and the quantity of writing fitted into the daily schedule of the writer. There was an experiment with audio-recording, but this was not repeated because Campbell did not feel comfortable doing the recording. Other communications (letters) were also included as the final diary data.

As mentioned above, the main finding of Campbell's study was that she made progress learning Spanish by using the language in situations where meaningful communication took place, particularly with friends, in the town, in bars, in her family environment, and outside of the classroom with the Mexican teachers. Campbell ended up dating one of the teachers and this increased her practice opportunities dramatically. The following is an example of what her diary entries looked like:

> Week 5: There were plenty of positive aspects to the evening at the Piano Bar in terms of language learning. I heard a lot of slang and fillers that I haven't gotten anywhere else. Maybe I could pick some up if I had more of the input. I did have to talk a lot in Spanish, like to Alberto and Mari's brother. And with Tito [her boyfriend] I spoke Spanish and he often spoke English, but not all the time. I spoke English only when I had a difficult verb structure coming up—past modals, counterfactual conditionals, etc. I commented at one point on how I was speaking Spanish and he English, and he said it was fun. And it's true, it was fun. It wasn't at all a fight about what to speak. It was okay that we were speaking different languages. It was that I speak Spanish slowly and he English slowly. (p. 211)

3.2.2 Language Learning Histories

Whereas diary studies are typically introspective accounts of learning in process, *language learning histories* (LLHs) are retrospective accounts of past learning. They are the written stories of language learning experiences. Benson (2011) points out that "the word history suggests a long-term account, although the periods of time covered by LLHs can vary greatly, ranging from the entire period over which a person has learned a language to much shorter periods, such as a year or semester of study or an incident that lasts no more than a few minutes" (p. 548). For this reason he prefers to term *language learning careers*, which applies to the entire period over which individuals have learned a language. However, for the sake of consistency, we use LLHs in this discussion. Our concern in this chapter is how to go about obtaining written data which tells a learner's history. We use as our featured illustrative study one that was carried out in university English-learning contexts in Japan and Taiwan (Murphey, Chen, and Chen, 2004).

BOX 3.2

Murphey, et al. (2004) were interested in first-year university students' social constructions of their identities as English learners. They wanted to discover if and how they invested in their learning and also in their imagined communities. Drawing on the work of Norton (2001), they use the term *imagined communities* to refer to the communities of practice that learners "see, or imagine, themselves belonging to in the present or the future" (p. 84). In their study they aimed to explore the connections among the learners' personal identities, imagined communities, and their investment in learning English, believing that doing so would have important consequences for the learners (by gaining more control of their own learning), their co-learners (by sharing and reading each others' LLHs), and for their teachers (by teaching more appropriately after reading the LLHs and learning about their learners). Data for the project consisted of learners' first-person narratives of their learning: i.e., their language learning histories. The students came from one university in Japan (84 students) and another in Taiwan (58 students). A thematic analysis was carried out on the written LLH data. The LLHs were successful in enabling the researchers to achieve their goals, that is, to determine "degrees of identification or non-identification and investments with imagined communities" (p. 86).

Writing the LLHs was a course assignment, and thus written mainly for the eyes of their teacher, although they were shared with fellow students (see below). Students were required to write a paper about their LLH from when they began to learn English to the present time and also about their thoughts on future learning. The length was to be about 750 words. The LLH had to be proofread (and signed and dated) by two classmates. The teacher offered students the option of submitting their work by email. The instructions for the LLH included suggestions for content that might be included, in the form of the following guiding questions (Murphey, et al., 2004: 86):

1. How did you learn English in Junior High School and High School?
2. What positive and negative experiences did you have and what did you learn from them?
3. What were you expecting before you came to the university?
4. What were you surprised about in your university classes?
5. How have you changed your ways of language learning since coming to the university?
6. What are the things that you found especially helpful?
7. What are the areas that you still want to improve in?
8. How do you think your next three years will be?
9. What are your language learning plans and goals after graduation?
10. What advice would you give to next year's first-year students?

The intentions of this set of questions are clear. They elicit narrative data that are temporal (reflecting on the past and looking to the future), emotive (positive and negative experiences, surprises), reflective (beliefs, expectations, and practices), strategic (plans and goals), and instructive (advice).

To illustrate the content and writing style of the LLHs we now present a few short excerpts. The thematic analysis conducted by the researchers revealed varying degrees of student identification with imagined communities. Following is an excerpt from the LLH of a student who lacked an imagined community with which to identify and ended up hating learning English:

> After class, I listened to the cassette for many times in order to memorize the sound of the words. It was a difficult job for me to do. I did so not because I accepted English, but because I didn't want to bring shame on myself . . . In short, when it comes to English, I was fear to speak and I hate to learn. (p. 88)

Others not only imagined future communities, but also saw themselves as successful members of those communities: "I started studying English at a private school, and I dreamed to be like my teacher because she told me many interesting stories which she had experienced in foreign countries" (p. 90). Often, experiences lead to de-investing in learning, for instance, when students achieve poor grades or are criticized by their teachers. However, other incidents have the opposite effect, encouraging learners to identify themselves more readily as English *users*:

When I took bus home, I met a foreigner and I come to him and spoke with him in English for a little while, although I knew my English was poor, that man encouraged and said, 'You have great English.' I was happy. When I got home I was grateful for him because he gave something I wanted for a long time. He made me like English. (p. 94)

Murphey, et al. (2004) argue that critical incidents such as these can create investments in learning. Further investment may occur as a result of learners' metacognitive awareness of their own learning gained through the process of writing their LLHs. Doing the writing means the learners are reflecting on who they are as learners, what contributes to and inhibits their learning, and how they can best progress in the future. As one student explains:

Before I start introducing my English language learning history, I want to tell you it is certainly helpful for me to understand what I have learned in English since beginning to get in touch with it and what my goals and plans are in the future. If you don't assign this homework I will never think these important things about myself. It is surely a great chance for me to know my attitude for English. (p. 96)

The set of ten questions used by Murphey, et al. (2004) proved to be very successful in generating the type of LLH data they were looking for. In fact they have been used in other studies as well. Barcelos (2008), for example, used the same questions in her study of learner beliefs about the place where they studied English (public school versus private English courses) and how these beliefs influenced their learning experiences. Tse (2000) also used ten questions in her study of adult university students' perceptions of their foreign language learning in the US and of the instructional methods used in foreign language courses. These questions are different from those of Murphey, et al. (2004) in that they elicit wholly retrospective accounts of learning, i.e., they do not ask participants to imagine future learning. Further differences, as one would expect, reflect the nature and topic of the research questions. Tse calls the written products autobiographies, though they could just as well have been called LLHs.

The questions prompted writing about the contexts of the students' learning experiences as well as, more specifically, sustained reflection on their actual experiences, attributions of success or failure, and any emotional issues. Their autobiographies were limited to five double-spaced pages, and they were instructed to be as specific and explicit as possible. The following are the questions they were given:

1. Which languages have you tried to learn?
2. How proficient are you in these languages? Are you able to speak, read, write them?

3. Where did you study these languages (e.g., study abroad, FL class), during what time in your life, for how long?
4. What were your reasons for studying these languages?
5. What types of activities or lessons were common in these classes?
6. What are some positive and negative aspects of studying a language this way?
7. How successful were you in acquiring the languages?
8. What contributed to your success/lack of success? Why?
9. How do you feel about learning languages as a result of your experiences?
10. What would you change about language classes to make them more effective?

The writers were asked to respond to all of the questions, though they could emphasize those which they felt were more appropriate to their own particular learning experiences. A further point to note about Tse's study is that the participants did not write the LLHs as part of a class project or assignment. They did so for the researcher's study—quite different, then, in terms of purpose and implications from the Murphey, et al. (2004) study.

3.2.3 Teacher Narratives

So far in this chapter our focus has been on the written narratives of language learners. We now turn to some examples of teacher writing. As we pointed out at the start of the chapter, some of these narratives are constructed for the purposes of professional development (typically some sort of reflection on practice), usually as a requirement for a course activity or assignment. These are then used by the writers, or their instructors, or both collaboratively, as data for a research project. Sometimes teachers (pre-service or in-service) write narratives specifically for the purposes of a study, usually their instructor's or an external researcher's.

In almost all cases, the written product is a teacher journal, that is, written reflections on teachers' practices, teaching contexts, emotions, development, and language learning. The purpose of these journals is for teachers to reflect on their own experiences of teaching and learning to teach; "*how* teachers come to know as well as *what* they come to know" (Golombek and Johnson, 2004: 312). These topics are also of interest to researchers, and so it is inevitable that teacher journals as narrative data are widely used in research on language teaching, particularly aspects of teacher education and identity.

Published studies which use narrative journal data are not always explicit about how the data were collected. For example, Tsui (2007) says in her narrative inquiry of the identity construction of an EFL teacher in China that the participant maintained "reflective diaries which he wrote for himself and shared with me. These reflections were further reshaped and enriched as I responded to his diaries by sharing my own experiences and probing for more information" (p. 659). We learn nothing more about the nature, form, or length of these diaries, or how the "probing" was effected. Nevertheless, the data collected were obviously rich and relevant since the published report on the study is a very readable, informative document which makes a worthy contribution to our understanding of teacher identity formation in the Chinese context. Table 3.1 summarizes a selection of narrative studies (including Tsui's) with varying degrees of explicit description of their data collection procedures, including instructions for how to go about writing the journals. The topics vary, as do the contexts, but all draw on teacher written journals as their main source of data. We now look more closely at Sakui's (2002) study.

BOX 3.3

Sakui (2002), a teacher of English in a Japanese university, was interested in investigating the relationship between her English learning and her teaching. Specifically, she wanted to illuminate how her learning experiences influenced her beliefs and practices in her language teaching. Her data included written journal entries as well as epiphanies in her learning and life experiences. A thematic analysis of the data (coding for themes and grouping these into broader categories) revealed a number of complex interconnected issues in her language learning and teaching life related to, for example, language acquisition, learner development, teacher beliefs, and teacher education. Sakui concluded by raising questions about the usefulness and legitimacy of her approach to autobiographical narrative inquiry, including narrative research reporting.

Here we have a teacher exploring her own language learning and teaching experiences for the purposes of professional development. Sakui produced written narrative data, which she analyzed. She then wrote a report based on her inquiry and this was subsequently published. Her data consisted of the following:

1. Self-reflective journal entries

   a. written over a period of six months during one academic semester;
   b. covered whatever topics Sakui felt were important or interesting, particularly related to her own personal knowledge and rationale for her teaching practices;
   c. not written for a specific purpose;
   d. twenty-nine entries were produced, which varied in length;
   e. about fifty pages in total.

2. Autobiographical account

   a. covered learning, life, and professional experiences;
   b. included epiphanies or critical events which were highlighted for further analysis and comment.

TABLE 3.1 Summary of studies using teacher journals as written data

Researcher	Aim	Participant(s)	Teacher journals	Narrative context	Other data
Tsui (2007)	To explore the complex process of identity formation (as an English language learner and teacher) of a practicing teacher in a Chinese university.	One male teacher, Minfang, covering a six-year period of learning and teaching English.	*Minfang's journals were personal reflective diaries that he shared and discussed with the researcher over a period of six months. Their collaboration meant that the diaries were shaped and re-shaped as their dialogue continued.*	The diaries were not produced for the purposes of a course assignment. They were for personal professional development. Tsui analyzed the data and wrote the report of the findings.	• Initial face-to-face storytelling when Minfang and Tsui met at a conference. • Four, four-hour face-to-face conversations over a period of one week at the end of the data-collection period.
Poon (2008)	To discover whether it is possible to employ action research as a means of professional development in the rapidly changing educational context of Hong Kong.	Three primary school teachers with no subject-specific (i.e., English) training or qualifications.	*Teachers each participated in an action research intervention in which they tried out new teaching methods. They "were encouraged to reflect on different aspects of their teaching, for instance, whether the lesson was effectively run and well received by the students, what problems were encountered, how to resolve the problems, how to improve teaching and learning, etc."* (p. 49)	The journals were written for the purposes of the action research projects, and thus for the professional development of the teachers involved. However, the action research projects were themselves part of a larger study by Poon, an independent researcher.	• Pre- and post-study interviews. • Pre- and post-lesson conferences. • Classroom observation. • Pre- and post-study interviews with three students.

Study	Purpose	Participants	Data	Notes	Analysis
Barkhuizen (2008a)	To investigate the use of narrative inquiry to explore the concept and relevance of context in language teaching.	Two teachers (the only two in the class) in an intensive graduate course on recent issues in language teaching in South Africa. One teacher had 20 years teaching experience and the other was pre-service.	*The teachers were required to write a series of three personal narratives of about 1000 words each in the space of a month. Three topics were suggested to provide some focus to the narratives:* 1. *Introduce yourself and tell the story of your interest in English teaching.* 2. *What are your ideas regarding the process of becoming a language teacher – generally, as well as personally?* 3. *What are some of the desires, fears, concerns, moments of joy that language teachers experience?* (p. 234)	The three narratives were written for the purposes of professional development (i.e., to reflect on the teachers' contexts of teaching and learning), and ultimately for a class assignment (they were to be analyzed). They were also used by the researcher to investigate the effectiveness of narrative inquiry for teacher reflection.	• Teachers' and the instructor's narratives were shared and discussed in class. • Ideas generated by the narratives were integrated with relevant theory and readings in class. • The teachers wrote assignments, which were reports of the analysis of their narratives.
Liu and Xu (2011)	To investigate how an EFL teacher in a university in China negotiates her identity in the face of significant pedagogical reforms.	One new university teacher of English. She was a recent graduate and the youngest member of the department.	*Data were collected over a period of two years. Written narratives took two forms:* 1. *Three reflective reports written in English to summarize her experience at different times of the academic year.* 2. *Reflective journals written in English throughout the year. Ongoing interpretations during analysis and journal writing were shared and discussed with the teacher.*	The reflective reports and journal entries were written expressly for the research. Professional contact with the teacher was maintained after the study had been completed.	• The researchers interviewed the teacher three times, each interview lasting 90 minutes. • Informal conversations and emails were also used, though not systematically analyzed.

Sakui's published article re-tells the story of her learning and teaching life experiences. At first, she focuses particularly on her learning and use of English, pointing out her competencies and limitations. She sums up her findings by referring to a metaphor for herself which emerged during her narrative self-reflections, that of Swiss cheese, the type of cheese with holes:

> I can carry out many activities and tasks in English without many problems, i.e. I possess a fairly large chunk of cheese as my abilities, but I cannot deny the constant awareness that my L2 language abilities are accompanied by shortcomings, the holes. (p. 142)

It is worth repeating that teachers' written narratives are produced in different research contexts, although reflective journal writing for the purposes of a course assignment or for an independent researcher's study are common. What the journals are about and how they are produced also vary enormously. For example, the topic of the journal could be:

1. Teachers' general reflections about their:
   a. teaching context, including the classroom, school, community, and wider socio-political context;
   b. instructional practices;
   c. learners' learning;
   d. philosophy of language teaching and learning;
   e. professional responsibilities and development.
2. Directly related to the content of a course they are taking.
3. Focused on the aims and research questions of a researcher.

The procedures for constructing the journals will need to take into account the following questions:

1. How many journal entries will the teacher construct?
2. How frequently will they be written?
3. How long will each entry and the entire journal be?
4. Over what period of time will it be written?
5. What topics will be covered (see above)?
6. What will the teachers do with them?
   a. analyze them for a course assignment;
   b. hand them over to a researcher for analysis;
   c. collaborate in the analysis with a researcher.
7. Who is the audience of the narratives, and the report, if an analysis is carried out?

One problem teachers often experience writing reflective journals is that they are unfamiliar with the genre and so struggle to know what to write and how to write it, even with guiding questions from an instructor or researcher. The same applies to language learners. One way of overcoming this problem is to structure even further the writing process. The next section introduces one means of doing so, the narrative frame.

3.2.4 Teacher and Learner Narrative Frames

A narrative frame is a written story template consisting of a series of incomplete sentences and blank spaces of varying lengths. It is structured as a story in skeletal form. The aim is for respondents to produce a coherent story by filling in the spaces according to their own experiences and their reflections on these. Frames "provide guidance and support in terms of both the structure and content of what is to be written. From the researcher's perspective the frames ensure that the content will be more or less what is expected (and required to address the research aims) and that it will be delivered in narrative form" (Barkhuizen and Wette, 2008: 376). Designing the frames can be somewhat of a challenge, mainly because they need to be structured in story form, when completed they should be read as a coherent whole, and they should require respondents to draw and reflect on their experiences of whatever the topic of the frames is. Poorly designed frames can result in random, unconnected responses to prompts that could just as well have been elicited by a questionnaire.

BOX 3.4

Barkhuizen and Wette (2008) introduce an approach to collecting written narrative data from teachers using narrative frames. To illustrate the concept and practice of using frames they drew on data collected from college English teachers in China during a professional development program they were involved in. They were interested in learning about the teaching and research experiences of the teachers in these particular regional and institutional contexts (see also Barkhuizen, 2009; Wette and Barkhuizen, 2009). Four narrative frames templates were designed and distributed to the more than 200 teachers at regular intervals during the two-week program. The topics covered by the frames included their language teaching background, research engagement, experience with curriculum development, and assessment practices. In their article the authors present illustrative findings relating to the teachers' engagement with research in their work environments. They conclude by discussing the strengths and limitations of the narrative frames approach to collecting written narrative data.

One of the frames is reproduced in Figure 3.1. In this case, the frame consists of sentence starters followed by blank spaces for the teacher's responses (see also Barnard and Nguyen, 2010, for an example on teachers' beliefs about task-based teaching). The aim of this frame was to elicit from teachers some background information about their training and their classroom practice, reflecting the content of what was covered in the professional development program in China: e.g., the issue of teachers' power in the classroom. Note the temporal dimension of the narrative, starting in the past (training), moving to the present (current practice), and looking to the future (imagining change). The aim of this design was to gather information about the teachers' experiences together with their reflections on these in story form. The question is: What is the structure of a story? Barkhuizen and Wette (2008) drew on the oft-quoted claim that a story has a beginning, a middle, and an end, and, where appropriate, incorporated into the frame Labov's (1972) narrative elements: abstract, orientation, complicating action, resolution, evaluation, and coda. A second frame focused on the teachers' research engagement. The sentence starters for this frame were as follows (p. 377):

1. I remember once in my classroom I had a very difficult time trying to . . .
2. The main reason for this problem was that . . .
3. I tried to solve the problem by . . .
4. It would have been very helpful if . . .
5. In relation to this difficulty, the type of research I'd like to do would . . .
6. The aim of the research would be to . . .
7. A major constraint, though, might be that . . .

Again, you can notice the temporal dimension in this frame, as well as the directed focus on one case (i.e., one problem in the classroom), and invitations for related reflections or evaluations.

Eighty-three complete sets of frames were collected. For each of the four frames, each teacher's written responses to the starters were combined into one story which represented that teacher's experiences and reflections. There were eighty-three separate stories for each of the four frames. By means of a content analysis, commonalities among teachers were then sought in the data. Barkhuizen and Wette (2008) report illustrative findings from the research methodology frame. In Barkhuizen (2009), which analyzes the teacher research data in more detail, these lists of categories (and their subthemes) were counted and ranked in terms of significance in the lives of the teachers.

Strengths associated with the use of the narrative frame include:

1. Those unfamiliar with self-reflective writing find it difficult, especially for the first time, and particularly when not writing in one's first language. The narrative frames enable respondents to write narratively by scaffolding them through the specially designed narrative structure.

I am an English teacher. The best thing about my teacher training was that _____

_____

_____

_____. When I first started to teach, _____

_____

_____

_____. The place

where I now teach is _____

_____

_____. My students are _____

_____

_____.

In my own classroom, I have the power to _____

_____

_____

_____. Making changes to my

teaching practice is something that _____

_____

_____. This is probably because _____

_____

_____. In the future, I am going to try to

_____.

FIGURE 3.1 A sample narrative frame (used in the study by Wette and Barkhuizen, 2009).

2. The design of the frames ensures that researchers obtain the information they want in order to achieve the aims of their study. However, there is still some flexibility in what the respondents actually write.

3. The spatial and structural restrictions do allow the narrators to tell their stories of experience: not long, detailed stories, but nevertheless storied snapshots of the respondents' life which, together with stories of other participants in similar contexts, is informative and relevant for the researcher.
4. The structured nature of the data makes for easier analysis.
5. The frames limit the quantity of data that is collected; therefore, the sample of respondents can be much larger than is typically found in narrative research.
6. Frames serve an exploratory purpose. They are useful for entry into a new research context (regional, social, cultural, educational, etc.).

And some limitations include:

1. The process of writing the frames may frustrate some writers who may need or desire more space.
2. The content structure of the frames (i.e., the narrative sequence of prompts) may not be compatible with the way a particular writer would like or be able to structure his or her own story.
3. Researchers may feel that at times they would like more content than that captured in the spaces available between prompts.
4. There is no opportunity for respondents to write about other (non-framed) topics.
5. There may be prompts which are interpreted in a way not intended by researchers.
6. The potential exists for narrators to write a list of unconnected ideas in response to the prompts if the frames are poorly designed or the instructions are not clear.
7. Ironically, the narrative frames tend to de-personalize the participants' stories of experience when combined and analyzed together with many other completed frames.

The narrative frames used in the Chinese teachers' project were of one type only: sentence starters serving as prompts. Frames could be constructed in a number of different ways (Barkhuizen and Wette, 2008: 384): (a) allowing more or unlimited space after sentence starters, (b) using prompts other than sentence starters, such as key words, mid- or end-sentence fragments, a sequence of time or place references, or any combination of these, (c) providing even less space in tightly controlled frames, and (d) supplying only the opening and closing sentences/paragraphs of a story.

Narrative frames have also been used to gather written data from language *learners* (see Macalister, 2012, who designed frames for the purpose of needs analysis in the process of curriculum design). Barkhuizen (2008b) used a frame to collect data on the English learning problems and successes of migrants and refugees in New Zealand. In designing the frame he took into account the problem of there not always being enough space to satisfy respondents who wish to write more. He therefore included in the design an empty box (with appropriate prompts) at the beginning and end of the actual sentence-starter frame for respondents to write freely any additional information they wished to share. Figure 3.2 shows one completed frame. The sentence starters are in italics. Notice that the frames are divided into *in the past, now* (the present), and *in the future*, and they aim to generate examples of learner problems and successes—real and imagined.

Narrative frames could also be used in combination with other data-collection instruments, such as demographic questionnaires, follow-up narrative interviews, journal writing, and classroom observation. Frames could form the core or primary data, but they are more likely to be suitable for initial exploration of research participants or sites.

3.3 Problems and Ethical Issues

In Chapter 2 we addressed a number of problems and ethical issues related specifically to collecting interview data and to narrative data more generally. Some of these issues are applicable to written narrative data as well. However, there are those which seem to be more relevant to narratives that take a written form. Perhaps the main problem is getting participants to write in the first place. From our experience of participating in research projects and of requiring learners and teachers to write in formal educational contexts (language classrooms and teacher education courses, respectively) we are aware that sometimes motivation to put pen to paper is not always high, and securing participation can be difficult. Participants are generally more willing to agree to engage in interviews.

When participants do write, however, they should be informed before writing starts that what they write is to be used for research purposes. When we tell stories, spoken or written, we do so with an audience in mind. There are things we tell some people but not others. So, when participants are asked to write journals, diaries, or LLHs, they should be informed in advance who the audience will be: e.g., their instructor (who may be the researcher), an independent researcher, conference attendees, and readers of published academic reports. For language learners, this is important when the writing is for classwork or assessment, for example, writing an LLH assignment. And the same applies for teachers' writing, for example, reflective journals during a professional development course. In these cases, the writing is normally very personal, and writers may get caught up in the process of completing an assessment or a course requirement, forgetting for the time being that what they are writing will later be used for research. Participants should be reminded of this purpose throughout the writing process, and perhaps most important, once their data have been analyzed the draft report should be provided to them for scrutiny.

Your story Part 1

I come from Iran. I speak Farsi and Turkish. Now also English. My arrival date was 2.10.2005. We, my husband and my daughter, live in Tauranga. My daughter is 7 years old. In Iran, lives my father and mother, 3 brothers and 3 sisters, and one nephew. My job in Iran, I was a dental nurse. Now in NZ I study English and take care of my family. Sometimes I take care of my friends' children. I have a small garden. My husband chose to come to NZ. My daughter likes NZ.

Your story Part 2

In the past

When I first came to NZ my English was almost non-existent. I could only say some of the alphabet, and hello and goodbye. *Soon after I arrived, a problem I experienced with English was* everything. I couldn't understand, or read or speak. I was worried about a lot of things. *Another problem I had with my English was* I wanted to understand, but I couldn't. I would like to work but I couldn't. *After a while, however,* I had been attending [name of institution] ESOL free classes. Fortunately I had made a friend. She could speak Farsi well and I had an ESOL Tutor. So gradually I began to understand. Also my daughter helped me. *I realized things were getting better when I was able to* hear words and understand some of them, and I could talk a little. *In those early days, another example of success with my English was* going shopping, and to understand the name, the price, and which size, which country the product came from.

Now

Now my English is a lot better. I can read - basic English, write, understand more than I can speak. *I find I can more easily* listen and understand people. *What I can really do well when I use English is* my pronunciation is very clear and reading is easier for me. *Also, I remember once* I bought my daughter some shorts, they were too small, so the lady explained to me to check the size, and small, medium and the age on the label. *However, when I use English I'm still having problems with* my ability to use English to express myself. *I would like to be able to solve this problem by* I think I need to talk more with different people. It is easier to talk with children, they use simpler words and sentences.

In the future

In the future, I would like to use English to return to work as a dental nurse. *I imagine that I will also be able to* become a beautician. *I will know that I have learned enough English when I* can understand and speak everything. *Learning English is important for me because* already I was 33 when I began studying English. Everyone speaks English here. It is important to learn this language.

Your story Part 3

After about one year my daughter told me, "Mum your English is getting better." Sometimes when I went out people wanted to talk to me, but I couldn't understand them, I just looked and they would talk a lot and then get tired and go away. It made me feel sad. But now I say "please speak less."

FIGURE 3.2 A completed narrative frame (Barkhuizen, 2008b).

Usually, institutions where researchers work (particularly universities) have their own ethics approval procedures for research involving "human participants," and many of these concerns would be addressed through that process. But many do not. Furthermore, some researchers are not affiliated with research institutions (like primary and secondary schools) and do not have supportive guidelines for how to go about requesting and securing informed consent from their research participants. These researchers would need to establish their own means of engaging participation ethically.

3.4 Conclusion

This chapter has presented examples of a number of different types of narrative data produced by language teachers and learners, including diaries, language learning histories, reflective teacher journals, and narrative frames. The first part of the chapter outlined various contexts in which such narratives are written for the purposes of inquiry. This was followed by a description of example studies which illustrate the narrative data types constructed in these contexts. In each case the data, as well as the data-collection procedures, were described in the hope that they serve an instructive purpose for readers. We concluded the chapter with a brief discussion of some of the challenges and ethical issues researchers face when working with written narrative data.

4

MULTIMODAL NARRATIVES

4.1 Introduction

Using multimodal narratives as data is a growing trend in narrative inquiry. In narrative research, researchers tend to use primarily a single source of narrative data, for example, oral (Chapter 2) and written (Chapter 3). In this chapter, we are concerned with the use of additional text types, other than oral or written, as narratives. We will first look at two examples from literacy studies. American cartoonist Lynda Barry published her literacy autobiography, *One Hundred Demons* (2002), as a way to address personal and social issues. The form that she chose was the graphic novel. In Barry's work, different objects (e.g., origami, newspaper cuttings, pressed flowers, etc.) are used to supplement cartoons. The result is a graphic novel, containing colorful collages and Zen Ink paintings, that tells the story of her literacy development from childhood to adulthood. Since its publication, Barry's work has been used as teaching and learning material in both literacy classes and teacher education in North America. Barry is a professional cartoonist, thus in her literacy autobiography, drawing and visual texts are centrally positioned in her work.

Jim Porter's (2002) text-based literacy autobiography examines his literacy development between 1960 and about 1995, and he placed technology as the catalyst for change. His essay includes photographs of different writing tools from ballpoint pens to early computing systems to personal computers. He argues that composing with technology, in multimodal form, and then presenting the outcome through networked computers, places writing in relevant social, pedagogical, and rhetorical contexts. When producing multimodal literacy narratives in the computer era, both the writing *medium* and the writing *environment* are different (Porter, 2002). Porter, for example, inserted photographs of changing technology into his writing to demonstrate the changing medium of writing.

The literacy narratives by Barry and Porter both included visual components to complement and enrich their written narrative texts. In language learning research, also, we have begun to see the use of multimodal narrative texts as alternatives or supplements to the more traditional written and spoken narratives covered in the previous two chapters. Multimodal texts can be used as subject (e.g., Barry, 2002) or as tool (e.g., Porter, 2002). As subject, the multimodal text is meant to be the end product and is the main set of data for narrative analysis. This is similar to the collection of written data for analysis, with additional photographs or drawings or hyperlinks inserted. As tool, the multimodal text is used as an artifact during interviews, in which the author (usually a language learner) discusses language learning with reference to the multimodal text. Here, the multimodal text is a prop, and it may or may not be analyzed independently. Compared to oral and written elicitation, the number of narrative analysis studies adopting multimodal texts either as subject of investigation or tools for investigation is comparatively small. However, there is a growing number of studies which are based on multimodal narratives in second language education. In this chapter, we look at digital and non-digital multimodal texts as subjects of and tools for narrative inquiry in language teaching and learning.

4.2 Contexts in which Multimodal Narrative Texts are Used

This chapter is concerned with multimodal data collection in narrative inquiry. We adopt Kress's definition of mode as that of "culturally and socially produced resources for representation" (2005: 6). Kress gives the examples of image, writing, music, layout, and others as different modes that people use to make and communicate meanings. Therefore, in this chapter, we consider narratives constructed by more than one mode as multimodal narratives; for instance, written narratives embedded with hyperlinks or photographs, or oral narratives supported or supplemented by photographs. In addition, "multimedia text" has been used by narrative researchers, a term used frequently in Computer-Assisted Language Learning research. Beatty (2010) defines multimedia texts as texts that include several media types; e.g., text, images, sound, or video. Multimedia text embraces both "the non-linear organization of text" and "non-linear and multiple information formats" (p. 45). Throughout the chapter, we will use both terms interchangeably. Definitions aside, our main focus is on the different ways narrative researchers appropriate multimodal/multimedia texts for data collection in narrative research.

As in studies using oral and written data, multimodal data are produced and collected in different contexts. The following outlines in more detail the contexts in which such data are produced and collected. The studies chosen here are categorized according to two criteria: either the authors themselves used the term "multimodal" or "multimedia" to describe their data, or we deemed the data to be "multimodal" or "multimedia." Studies that have been referenced as examples are discussed in more detail later in the chapter.

A. Researchers produce multimodal texts about episodes of language learning and/or literacy practices (e.g., in school or at home) to create visual data in support of written narratives or to stimulate the production of narratives together with the participants. Multimodal texts frequently created and used are photographs or videos (photo-documentation). These texts are sometimes used as prompts during interviews or discussions (DaSilva Iddings, et al., 2005) or as supplementary visual narratives to support research findings arrived at by other means (Pahl, 2004).

B. Researchers ask language learners to produce multimodal texts to represent the language learning process and experience. These texts mainly come in two forms: photographs (Nikula and Pitkänen-Huhta, 2008) and drawings (Kalaja, et al., 2008; Dufva, et al., 2011). The photographs in Nikula and Pitkänen-Huhta (2008) were used as prompts for group discussion, and participants in Kalaja, et al. (2008) were asked to write a short text to explain their self-portrait drawings.

C. Researchers collect multimodal texts produced by language learners as products of classroom tasks in their regular learning environments. The texts in these studies included multilingual writing (Li, 2011), photographs and digital stories (Vasudevan, et al., 2010), text-based language learning histories (LLHs) with photographs and media hyperlinks (Menezes, 2008), and online multimedia LLHs (Chik and Breidbach, 2011a, 2011b).

D. Researchers collect multimodal texts produced by language learners as literacy products in home environments (photographs and drawings in Pahl, 2004, and Pietikäinen, et al., 2008) or in out-of-class literacy practices (blog entries in Lee, 2006).

The sections that follow showcase examples of studies that cover some of these possibilities. We first examine texts produced from visual elicitation methodology, and then multimedia LLHs produced for different online settings.

4.2.1 Visual Elicitation

Visual elicitation is used frequently in ethnographic research to provide stimuli for interviews and to provide insights into informants' perspectives (Pink, 2012). The visual texts used are usually photographs and drawings. Visual elicitation is included in this chapter because, first, it is a medium that shows potential for data collection in narrative research, and second, it offers the possibility of creating other forms of digital narratives (see for example, Lee, 2006 and Vasudevan, et al., 2010). In narrative research, both photographs (Nikula and Pitkänen-Huhta, 2008) and drawings (Kalaja, et al., 2008) have been used as stimuli for interviews. In a study of Korean-American blogging in Korean, the participants embedded photographs to enrich or supplement the writing in their blog entries. Lee (2006) then uses screenshots of selected blog entries as stimuli for interviews and also for textual analysis of the

FIGURE 4.1 A Hong Kong secondary school student's self-portrait as an English learner.

participants' Korean learning. In a study by Vasudevan and her colleagues (2010), photographs taken by a Bengali girl who had recently arrived in the United States were made into a digital story of her cultural heritage. The digital story was then used to represent the LLH of this young learner, demonstrating progress in English use from the beginning of the project to the final presentation of the digital story. In a study with Hong Kong secondary school students learning German as a foreign language, Chik (forthcoming) asked students to draw portraits of themselves as English and German learners (see Figures 4.1 and 4.2) and to write a short explanation of the drawings. As can be seen in Figure 4.1, the student drew her English-learning self as a happy teenager wearing her daily clothes because she uses English in her daily life. But her German-learning self is seen wearing a school uniform, signaling that German learning is reserved for the classroom.

Nikula and Pitkänen-Huhta (2008) provide a good example of using participants' visual narratives to generate more in-depth oral discussion of language learning in both formal and informal contexts.

FIGURE 4.2 The same student's self-portrait as a German learner.

BOX 4.1

Nikula and Pitkänen-Huhta (2008) wanted to understand the role of English in Finnish teenagers' out-of-school lives. This study is part of a larger project on English in Finnish adolescents' everyday practices, which is based on the assumption that literacy is socially situated and language learner and user identities are constructed by "socially, culturally and historically bound practices" (p. 171). The researchers used photo elicitation as a research tool to record "subjective experiences with languages" and stimulate the teenagers to talk about their informal language learning outside school contexts. Nikula and Pitkänen-Huhta argue that the photographs highlighted two levels of narratives: stories of learning *in* and stories of learning *around* the photographs. Primary data for the study were interview data that recorded the participants' discussions of the photographs.

> The analysis shows that for these youth, everyday practices are "personally meaningful sites for informal learning," so much so that these practices are not viewed as learning.

Seven Finnish teenagers (four females and three males) in grades eight and nine joined the project on investigating the role of English in their everyday life and social practices. The participants were instructed to "take any number of photographs of situations, places and activities in their everyday surroundings where English in their view has some significance" (Nikula and Pitkänen-Huhta, 2008: 174). Each participant took a set of about ten photographs, amounting to about seventy photographs in total.

The photographs were broadly categorized into five types: travelling, entertainment, print media, computers, and hobbies. Nikula and Pitkänen-Huhta argued that these five categories represented the participants' encounters with and uses of English. They viewed photographs that included textbooks and dictionaries, indexing the social relevance and importance of English learning in Finnish society. This indexing also reflected the teenagers' identity construction as English language learners and users. In the report of the study, only four photographs were reprinted. These four photographs were divided into two sets: textbooks and dictionaries, and skateboarding and snowboarding. In the first set, learning objects and tools were shown. In the second set, each photograph showed a boy doing a trick with his skateboard or snowboard. In the sports photographs, it is clear that a third party took the photograph of the person skateboarding or snowboarding, thus indicating group activities.

After categorizing the photographs, Nikula and Pitkänen-Huhta conducted two separate group discussions with the boys and the girls to discuss "issues raised by the photographs" (p. 174). Attention was paid to linguistic features (for example, word choices and grammatical constructions) because these features grounded the discursive construction of identities. The photographs proved to have provided good talking points among the participants, and Nikula and Pitkänen-Huhta identified three themes: formal vs. informal learning, incidental learning, and gaining expertise through informal learning. Under each theme, excerpts from the conversations were used to illustrate the points. The content of the photographs were only briefly mentioned in the captions: "Photographs of school textbooks and a dictionary 'English-Finnish dictionary'" (p. 176) and "Photographs of skateboarding and snowboarding" (p. 181). Nikula and Pitkänen-Huhta argue that while photographs provided useful access to language learning as a personal experience and practice, the visual narratives in the photographs did not contrast learning in formal with informal contexts. However, the discussion did give the participants the opportunity to raise personal issues. Nikula and Pitkänen-Huhta conclude that the Finnish teenagers made a distinction between language *learning* in formal contexts and language *use* in informal contexts. At the same time, the participants also viewed themselves as experts in specific areas of language use, for instance, the boys' use of English skateboarding jargon. Nikula and Pitkänen-Huhta argue that this expert positioning through language learning and use in informal contexts indicates that language teachers may need to acknowledge the value of informal learning.

4.2.2 Multimedia Language Learning Histories

In Chapter 3, we discussed language learning histories (LLHs) as a written form of data. Here, we look at multimedia LLHs, which are retrospective accounts of past learning presented not only in writing, but also with images and/or sound.

BOX 4.2

Menezes (2008) was interested in the complexity of second language acquisition (SLA). Her study aimed to search for recurrent patterns in multimedia LLHs which show SLA as a complex system, and the ways different media components in the LLHs interact to construct this knowledge. She used the grammar of visual design developed by Kress and van Leeuwen (1996) to analyze multimedia texts. While Kress and van Leeuwen work primarily with visual components in multimodal texts, Menezes was more interested in sounds. She suggests that while "multimedia portray much more information than each individual medium does" (p.201), the interactions among different media allow the emergence of meaning. The study included thirty-seven multimedia LLHs composed by English language teachers and a LLH written by Menezes. The visual elements and compositions of most LLHs suggested a strong recognition and acknowledgement of the audience. Writers also included visual components and hyperlinks to web-based audio clips to highlight their out-of-class learning. These multimedia components highlighted the different ways individual learners *use* English language in these contexts. The analysis of LLHs has led researchers to become aware that SLA is a complex system and that people have different ways of learning. Menezes concludes her study by suggesting that the use of multimedia materials in these LLHs provides further value for readers to understand the complexity of the language learning process.

By using multimedia texts, Menezes (2008: 201) argues that "pictures and sounds not only illustrate written texts, but also make up a larger network of meanings." In her study, thirty-eight prospective Brazilian language teachers from an online course on computer literacy and English language skills enhancement composed multimedia LLHs as their final assignment. The students were told "to describe how they had learned English and to include hyperlinks, images and sounds" (p. 204). The LLHs were presented as Microsoft Word files with embedded photographs or graphics or hyperlinks, and were then circulated among students in a Yahoo Group. After the students circulated, commented on, and edited the LLHs, thirty-seven students gave their permission for publishing them on a project website (http://www.veramenezes.com/amfale/narmult.html). Menezes also interviewed one student via email to understand her choices of hyperlinks. These LLHs and the interview formed the corpus of her study.

Unlike Nikula and Pitkänen-Huhta (2008), who used photographs as tools to collect additional oral data, Menezes treated the multimedia LLHs as subjects of investigation. She conducted a textual analysis using the visual grammar framework of Kress and van Leeuwen (1996) and applied it to all the visual components present in the LLHs. Some images were discarded because Menezes did not have permission to publish them. She analyzed screenshots from different sections of the multimedia LLHs to determine the functions of the visual and audio components and their relationship to the textual components.

In their LLHs students divided their language learning experiences into formal and informal learning contexts and inserted media texts into the two different sections. Menezes categorizes the visual images into social action, transactional, reactional, mental, and verbal processes to highlight the agency of the learners in different contexts. In formal contexts, learners often showed that they were bored or had high levels of anxiety. In sections concerning out-of-class learning, students incorporated more visual and hyperlinks to pop music websites and other videos. The increased use of media texts is also linked to lowered levels of anxiety and greater control of their own learning. Menezes (2008) extends the visual grammar framework by including the analysis of audio components in the multimedia LLHs, and examples used in the study show that writers do show coherent grammatical use of the various multimedia components. Menezes argues that the use of multimedia components indicates that the second language acquisition process is a "dynamic non-linear process" (p. 206).

Menezes's (2008) study is among the few that treat multimedia narratives as subjects of investigation (see also Da Silva Iddings, et al., 2005, and Kalaja, et al., 2008). The study shows that the different ways writers employed multimedia components, for example, photographs, sound clips, and hyperlinks to external websites, enriched the retelling of the learning experiences. She also takes advantage of the sharable nature of multimedia files by sharing all the LLHs first in a private Yahoo Group, and later on a public-access website. The two-step procedure is a good model for a course structure. While the course was in progress, students shared their work freely among course members through a secure and private online platform, and allowed peer reviewing and reading of LLHs after class. Menezes points out that some students read other LLHs before writing their own evaluative conclusions. This illustrates the dynamic process of LLH composition, especially in linking the participants up through an online group, which is a less discussed aspect in narrative research. At the end of the course, Menezes reposted all but one LLHs to a public research website. At this point, any students and teachers with Internet access can read them. This global sharing of LLHs extends dialogue on foreign language learning in different contexts. We have used Menezes's collection of digital LLHs in different classes and workshops to stimulate conversation on foreign language learning in diverse cultural contexts.

One LLH in Menezes's study was not published on the public research website and some pictures were not analyzed and used because permission was not obtained. This raises issues of online privacy and research anonymity, which was addressed in the next featured study (Chik and Breidbach, 2011b).

4.2.3 Online Language Learning Histories and Group Discussion

Nikula and Pitkänen-Huhta (2008) used visual materials to conduct face-to-face group interviews. The study by Menezes (2008) shows the potential of sharing multimedia LLHs among teachers through a Yahoo Group. Chik and Breidbach (2011b) used multimedia LLHs to allow pre-service teachers and learners to share and respond to LLHs by interacting directly in an online environment.

BOX 4.3

Chik and Breidbach (2011b) explore the use of multimedia LLHs for intercultural exchange between Hong Kong and German students. The German students were pre-service English language teachers while the Hong Kong students were English majors. This study aimed to facilitate dialogue between students from different cultural and educational contexts and thus to promote reflection on their language learning pathways and development. The published article reports on two projects conducted between 2008 and 2010. Chik and Breidbach (2011b) used online platforms and Web 2.0 tools to facilitate the sharing of LLHs and interactions. The Hong Kong students first posted their multimedia LLHs on a project wiki site, and the German students uploaded their text-based LLHs. The participants exchanged comments through the wiki site. In the second cohort, the students first uploaded their LLHs to the project wiki site and conducted the first round of intercultural dialogue. Then, following the initiative of the Hong Kong students, a Facebook group and two Skype meetings were set up to replace the project wiki. The study showcased the challenges of sharing LLHs in the Web 2.0 era, especially in terms of interactivity and multimodality. The Hong Kong participants wanted to share LLHs and conduct online interaction through personal social media channels, but this suggestion was only welcomed by some of the German participants. The study concluded by pinpointing learning beyond the language classroom as a fruitful domain for future intercultural online LLHs projects.

In contrast to Menezes (2008), the study by Chik and Breidbach (2011b) was initiated as a long-term project for facilitating intercultural exchange for language teacher education between Hong Kong and German students. Given this aim, Chik and Breidbach designed the collection and sharing of multimedia LLHs on open online platforms. Once they had decided to create a collaborative project, their planning for interaction had to take into account the differences in semester structure and time zones. As the Hong Kong students started their autumn semester first, the team decided to ask them to begin preparation ahead of the late-October German semester start. The Hong Kong students were recruited from a general writing course, and one of the course assignments was the writing and presentation of a digital LLH. The steps the Hong Kong students followed to complete their LLHs were as follows:

1. Students in the course formed groups to set up their group wiki sites. A wiki is a collaborative web space, which allows easy editing, collaborative writing, and asynchronous commenting.
2. Students were given instructions to include more than one mode in their LLH. They uploaded multimodal LLHs to their group wiki (see Figures 4.3 and 4.4). While some LLHs were text-based with variation in font color and size, some included extensive embedding of popular cultural visual and/or media texts (see Figures 4.5 and 4.6).
3. Students read and commented on the LLHs as part of the assignment requirements.
4. At mid-course, a call for participation was announced and twelve students responded. The LLHs written by these twelve students were transferred to another project wiki site for sharing with the German participants.
5. By November 2008, twelve Hong Kong and four German students were involved in the research project.
6. The German students read the Hong Kong LLHs before composing their LLHs.
7. The German LLHs were more text-based. They were uploaded to the project wiki site.
8. The project wiki site included a comments section for all participants.
9. All Hong Kong and German participants shared project account logins.

10. Both Hong Kong and German participants read the LLHs written by the other group and submitted comments.
11. Participants took part in discussions among themselves and participated in a second round of commenting on the wiki site.

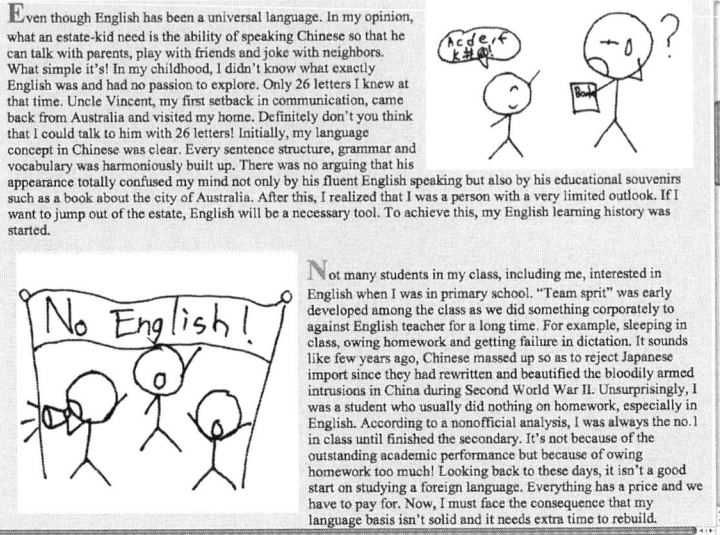

Even though English has been a universal language. In my opinion, what an estate-kid need is the ability of speaking Chinese so that he can talk with parents, play with friends and joke with neighbors. What simple it's! In my childhood, I didn't know what exactly English was and had no passion to explore. Only 26 letters I knew at that time. Uncle Vincent, my first setback in communication, came back from Australia and visited my home. Definitely don't you think that I could talk to him with 26 letters! Initially, my language concept in Chinese was clear. Every sentence structure, grammar and vocabulary was harmoniously built up. There was no arguing that his appearance totally confused my mind not only by his fluent English speaking but also by his educational souvenirs such as a book about the city of Australia. After this, I realized that I was a person with a very limited outlook. If I want to jump out of the estate, English will be a necessary tool. To achieve this, my English learning history was started.

Not many students in my class, including me, interested in English when I was in primary school. "Team sprit" was early developed among the class as we did something corporately to against English teacher for a long time. For example, sleeping in class, owing homework and getting failure in dictation. It sounds like few years ago, Chinese massed up so as to reject Japanese import since they had rewritten and beautified the bloodily armed intrusions in China during Second World War II. Unsurprisingly, I was a student who usually did nothing on homework, especially in English. According to a nonofficial analysis, I was always the no.1 in class until finished the secondary. It's not because of the outstanding academic performance but because of owing homework too much! Looking back to these days, it isn't a good start on studying a foreign language. Everything has a price and we have to pay for. Now, I must face the consequence that my language basis isn't solid and it needs extra time to rebuild.

FIGURE 4.3 A language learning history with cartoon drawing.

Secondary School

Since my examination results in Primary five and six were good, I was able to get into one of the best EMI Secondary school in my district. As a reward of my good academic performance and the need of my studies, my parents gave me a computer in Form one.

During my early secondary school, I occasionally went to play computer games in my friends' home. In the course of time, I became so indulged in these games that my first thing to do after school was to play computer games, and I would not start to do my homework until my mother came home. As the "side effect" of playing these games, I learnt the English names of countries and weapons, and read quite a bit about world history, especially in the "Age of Empires" series.

Age of Empires, Red Alert and Empire Earth were my favorite computer games. I learnt a lot of new vocabularies through these games.

FIGURE 4.4 A language learning history showcasing digital gameplay.

FIGURE 4.5 A language learning history with popular cultural texts.

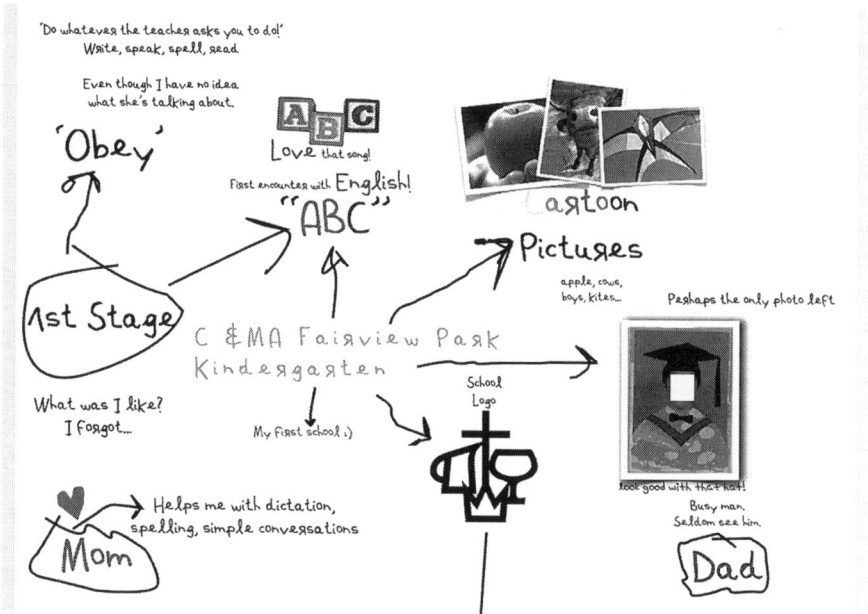

FIGURE 4.6 A language learning history written as a love letter.

The second, 2009 cohort consisted of seven Hong Kong undergraduate and eight German postgraduate students. These participants had completed all the same steps (Step 1 through 11) as the previous cohort, but this time the Hong Kong participants initiated the use of additional social media tools after one round of commenting:

1. The Hong Kong participants set up a closed Facebook group for the project with all the Hong Kong members added.
2. Some German participants responded positively and were added to the group.
3. Discussion was conducted through the Facebook group (Figure 4.7 and 4.8).
4. Two Skype video conferencing sessions were arranged through the Facebook group discussion.

Chik and Breidbach (2011b) comment on two dimensions of the projects: the content of the LLHs, and the technical aspects of using multimedia LLHs and Web 2.0 tools for intercultural exchange. The participants came from two different

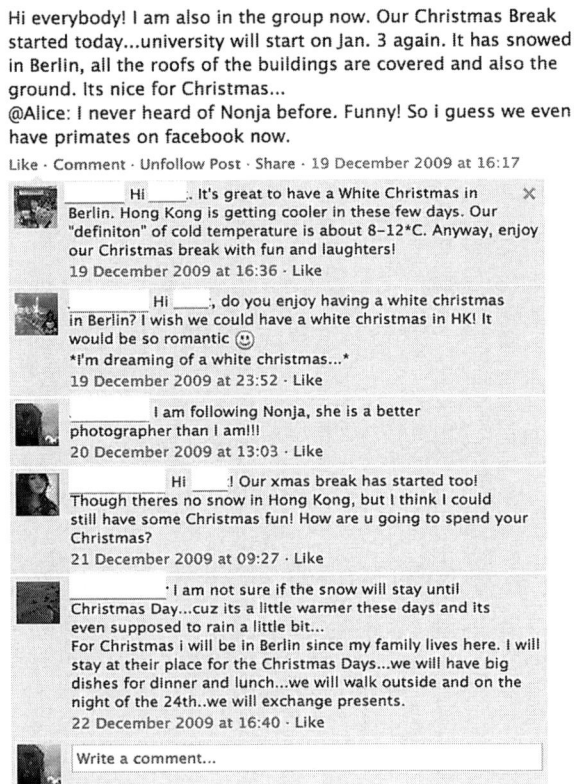

Hi everybody! I am also in the group now. Our Christmas Break started today...university will start on Jan. 3 again. It has snowed in Berlin, all the roofs of the buildings are covered and also the ground. Its nice for Christmas...
@Alice: I never heard of Nonja before. Funny! So i guess we even have primates on facebook now.
Like · Comment · Unfollow Post · Share · 19 December 2009 at 16:17

_____ Hi _____. It's great to have a White Christmas in Berlin. Hong Kong is getting cooler in these few days. Our "definiton" of cold temperature is about 8–12*C. Anyway, enjoy our Christmas break with fun and laughters!
19 December 2009 at 16:36 · Like

_____ Hi _____, do you enjoy having a white christmas in Berlin? I wish we could have a white christmas in HK! It would be so romantic 😊
I'm dreaming of a white christmas...
19 December 2009 at 23:52 · Like

_____ I am following Nonja, she is a better photographer than I am!!!
20 December 2009 at 13:03 · Like

_____ Hi _____! Our xmas break has started too! Though theres no snow in Hong Kong, but I think I could still have some Christmas fun! How are u going to spend your Christmas?
21 December 2009 at 09:27 · Like

_____· I am not sure if the snow will stay until Christmas Day...cuz its a little warmer these days and its even supposed to rain a little bit...
For Christmas i will be in Berlin since my family lives here. I will stay at their place for the Christmas Days...we will have big dishes for dinner and lunch...we will walk outside and on the night of the 24th..we will exchange presents.
22 December 2009 at 16:40 · Like

Write a comment...

FIGURE 4.7 Hong Kong and German participants interacted on the Facebook group.

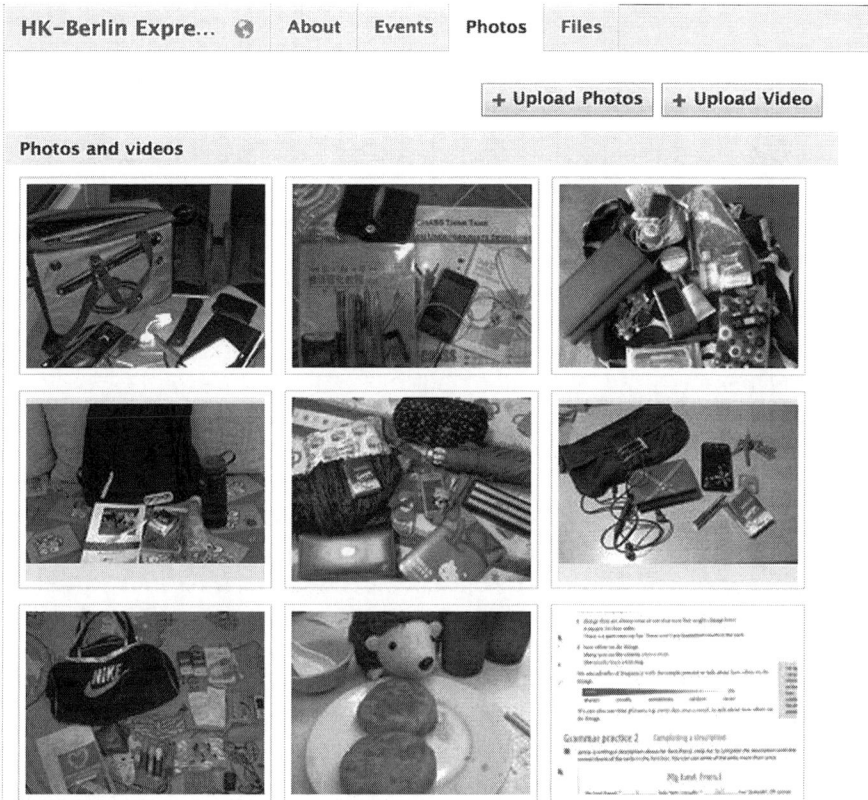

FIGURE 4.8 Hong Kong and German participants shared photographs on the Facebook group.

programs: The Hong Kong students were English-major undergraduates and the German students were pre-service, English teacher education postgraduates. The differences in identities influenced the ways the LLHs were composed. The Hong Kong LLHs mostly highlighted language learning and use beyond the classroom, thus including more photographs or popular cultural visuals or embedded YouTube music videos. Most of the German LLHs were solely text-based with a few containing a couple visuals, and they focused primarily on pedagogical evaluation of prior learning experiences. The focus on out-of-class learning and use by the Hong Kong participants might have been a blessing in disguise as both parties found new domains for discussion—English language popular cultural and media texts. Chik and Breidbach (2011b) argue that popular culture may provide the bridge for future intercultural projects on LLHs exchange.

Another direction of the discussion in the study focuses on the adoption of Web 2.0 social media for narrative research purposes, especially in terms of logistics and online privacy. The use of Web 2.0 social media tools may entail the disclosure of personal information (e.g., details of a Facebook account). Some participants did not feel comfortable joining and withdrew from the project. The use of a common project login might have provided a solution, but the traditional wisdom of research anonymity did not fit well with the Web 2.0 environment. The demand for privacy may also partially explain the sparse visual materials in the German LLHs. In the Hong Kong LLHs, students were happy to contribute personal and family photographs to demonstrate their out-of-class English learning experiences (e.g., travel photographs), but the German students appeared to be more sensitive about the issue, and were reluctant to post personal photographs.

The logistics of arranging intercultural exchange between groups with a time zone difference can also be a major hurdle for group interactivity. However, the use of a wiki and a Facebook group provided the convenience of asynchronous interaction at the participants' own pace. Chik and Breidbach (2011b) used a wiki site to encourage participants to upload, share, and co-edit LLHs. A wiki provides the possibility of convenient online collaboration through content editing and/or comments provision. In the end, the collaborative writing aspect was not utilized, but the participants did use the asynchronous commenting function, and they could respond to comments at their own pace. The commenting function suited participants living in different time zones.

While participants were comfortable using Microsoft Office for daily composition, adapting to new Web 2.0 tools required another level of technical learning. The Hong Kong participants were more familiar with the wiki operation because of prior academic exposure, and this provided them with a slight technological advantage, and they had higher expectations. The German participants had to catch up in a much shorter space of time, which accounted for their somewhat indifferent response to the integration of multimedia texts in their LLHs. The participants' dissimilar expectations also raise the question about the necessity or desirability of including multimedia components in online LLHs presentations. Given the ever-changing reading practices in online environments, will multimedia texts replace text-based narratives? For the popular cultural media texts, most were not original productions. Instead, the participants remixed and re-appropriated web-based sources. This may also require further discussion with regard to copyright issues.

As we adopt technology into narrative research, perhaps one future direction is the use of multimedia LLHs. The participants in Menezes (2008) composed their multimedia LLHs as Microsoft Word files, and then the files were circulated among the members of a Yahoo Group. The advantage of this arrangement was that the members were all from the same online course, and their interaction in the Yahoo Group was an extension of their academic study. In Chik and Breidbach (2011b), the LLHs were shared through a wiki and then interaction was conducted through the use of a common project login. There appears still to be a division between academic and personal worlds. The turn to a personal social media site (Facebook) meant crossing from an academic to a personal world. While this could add a new level of intimacy to the reading of LLHs, it might also create resistance.

4.3 Hosting Multimodal Language Learning Narratives

The studies by Menezes (2008) and Chik and Breidbach (2011b) indicate that the use of multimedia LLHs can be taken a step further for collaborative research purposes. The sharing of LLHs points to the need to consider the hosting and archiving of digital LLHs. In this section, we discuss briefly the structuring and technical aspects of multimodal data management. For illustrative purposes we refer to two websites which host collections of language learning narratives: the *Digital Archive of Literacy Narratives* (DALN, Cynthia Selfe and H. Lewis Ulman of Ohio State University) and *Aprendendo com Memórias de Falantes e Aprendizes de Língua Estrangeira* (AMFALE, "Learning from memoirs of foreign language learners and speakers," Vera Menezes of Universidade Federal de Minas Gerais). The two websites orient towards different readerships: DALN is set up for a general American audience, and Menezes's website is set up for second and foreign language learners and teachers. The different readership orientations provide insights into the construction and design of the websites as well as the narratives elicited, and thus warrant our attention in this section.

We begin with the American-based *Digital Archive of Literacy Narratives* (DALN). DALN is:

> a publicly available archive of literacy narratives in a variety of formats (print, video, audio) that together provide a historical record of the literacy practices and values of U.S. citizens, as these practices and values change. The DALN invites people of all ages, races, communities, backgrounds, and interests to contribute stories about how they learned to read, write, and compose meaning and how they continue to do so. (Selfe, C., & Ulman, H.L. (2013). *Digital Archive of Literacy Narratives*. Retrieved from http://daln.osu.edu/)

While members of the DALN consortium are educators and researchers, contributors came from all walks of life. With its clear mission of providing a historical record of the changing literacy practices in America, the website adopts an open door policy to narrative elicitation. The archive asks for a valid email address for membership registration and all users can contribute a narrative directly through the website. The archive also provides a *Do It Yourself* step-by-step guide for users to compose their audio and/or video literacy narratives. On the website, literacy narrative is specifically defined as "simply a collection of items that describe how you learned to read, write, and compose." Though literacy narratives are conventionally connected to one's first language, as was the case in Barry (2002) and Porter (2002), DALN contributors do not necessarily limit themselves to the discussion of learning in a first language. The archive was set up in 2008, and as of today, the collection contains more than 3000 literacy narratives, including the learning of English as a second language and the learning of modern and heritage languages. When searching the database with the key words "second language," 646 results were found. The TESOL Teachers section on the DALN Resource page contains sample texts, multimedia narratives and teaching materials, indicating the pedagogical and research potential of these multimedia narratives. The consortium has published their research findings based on the narratives on their website.

Although also hosting foreign language learning narratives, AMFALE is very different from DALN. Menezes compiled several collections of multimodal language learning narratives collected by second and foreign language teachers from different parts of the world. These collections included written narratives from Brazil (Ana Maria Barcelos and others), Finland (the ALMS team), and Japan (Tim Murphey). On her website, she also included audio (Vera Menezes) and multimodal narratives (Vera Menezes with Brazilian learners, and Alice Chik with Chinese learners). The large collection of LLHs allows us to see the representation of learning narratives in different cultures. All these researchers have informative and innovative research published based on these narratives, and several ongoing doctoral projects have also been developed (see Chik, forthcoming; Kalaja, et al., 2008; Menezes, 2008; Murphey and Carpenter, 2008).

The section on audio and multimodal texts provides differing access to the language learning narratives. The audio section, for example, paints an interesting picture of Brazilian learners of different foreign languages (English, French, German, Italian, and Spanish). The audio tracks are only available in Portuguese, however, which reflects a larger Brazilian audience. The multimodal texts collected by Vera Menezes and Alice Chik point to technological and structural differences in different digital technology eras. As explained in Menezes (2008), the multimodal LLHs composed by Brazilian learners were presented as Microsoft Word files with pictures and hyperlinks. These files were then shared among members through a Yahoo Group. Most of the multimodal texts were composed before 2008, prior to the wider availability of user-friendly Web 2.0 writing tools (e.g., blog and wiki). Chik's LLHs were written by university students in their composition classes for sharing on wiki platforms, with both embedded and hyperlinks to media texts (see Figures 4.1–4.4). After obtaining the permission of the students, Chik later migrated these multimodal narratives to a different wiki site for permanent hosting. Menezes's website hosts elicited LLHs and does not accept unsolicited LLHs, but its specific focus on second and foreign language learning provides greater ease of use for language educators.

4.4 Problems and Ethical Issues

The adoption of multimodal texts can present a number of potential problems and ethical issues. First and foremost, original multimodal narratives in academic publications, such as colorful drawings or color photographs, are reproduced in black and white. It is left up to the researchers' descriptions to give life to the multimodal presentation. In addition, the presentation of texts with hyperlinks and multimedia texts are shown as screen captures. This type of presentation does not allow the full appreciation of the original design and non-linear reading of the texts.

Rose (2012) points out that ethical issues associated with visual ethnographical studies are consent, anonymity, and copyright, and these are equally relevant to multimodal narrative inquiry. The issue of copyright for media texts used in visual and multimedia reports can be partly dealt with by using texts available from Creative Commons (creativecommons.org). Text creators can publish their work under the Creative Commons license, which gives the public free access to their work with or without conditions (for instance, only for non-commercial purposes). The Creative Commons website provides search options for different types of media texts: music (Jamendo, ccMixter, and SoundCloud), images (Flickr, Fotopedia, Google Images, Open Clip Art Library, and Pixabay), and video and media (Europeana, SpinXpress, Wikimedia Commons, and YouTube). Creative Commons is only one among other open source pools or archives. The Internet Archive (archive.org) also provides access to digital formats of historical collections that are in the public domain, thus allowing appropriation or adaptation by students.

Issues of consent are also related to the digital archiving of these multimodal texts. While participants may have given the researchers permission for their texts to be used for teaching or research purposes, the hosting of these texts online may present a new problem: online privacy. The requirement for human subject approval can become a tricky issue. In most narrative studies, regardless of the data elicitation methods, participants are frequently given the academic protection of anonymity, typically by the use of pseudonyms, or the removal of their name and personal details. However, this type of removal may not be as easily done in multimodal texts. For instance, in Chik's collection of multimodal LLHs, some writers created their LLHs as slideshows and YouTube videos, in which the participants usually contributed personal photographs of language learning. The most common types included sitting with a novel, or photographs taken during overseas study or leisure trips, or photographs with overseas friends. For these types of LLHs, it is almost impossible to remove the personal details without destroying the integrity of the texts.

A final ethical issue may be even more critical: the reprinting of multimodal narratives in publicly available journal articles and books. In Lee's (2006) report of her study of the blogging activities of two Korean American siblings she was very careful in her handling of the visual images and screen shots of the blog entries and other online activities. Lee states:

> No identifiable images and names of the informants were used, and all excerpts of the collected data were sent to the participants for their review and consent. Furthermore, as I was explaining the procedures and

the rights of the informants as participants in the study, I specifically inquired about their feelings toward using their language practices in Cyworld [a popular Korean blog and social networking site] as public research data. (p. 98)

Though protecting the anonymity of participants is standard procedure for all research projects, it may present a particular problem for the posting of visual materials. Interestingly, Lee adds that, "both informants stated that they felt comfortable sharing the information with others, because the content of their postings was about aspects of their life that they did not deem to be private" (p. 98). Our changing attitudes towards privacy in online environments may be progressing faster than institutional requirements on privacy protection.

The following checklist can be used as a helpful set of general guidelines when using multimodal narratives.

BOX 4.4

Checklist for Adopting Multimodal Narratives

Before making the decision to use multimodal texts, researchers should be familiar with the medium (e.g., the operation of the digital camera, the operation of a website, the production of a video, etc.). They should decide whether the multimodal texts will be used as the subjects of investigation or tools for additional data collection (e.g., interview or writing). As with other types of data collection, it is essential to design a consent form that requests permission to use selected images or screenshots for academic publications.

Equipment

Equipment plays a more important role in multimodal data elicitation than it does in oral and written data elicitation.

Photographs

1. If possible, provide participants with access to a camera. It can be a disposable or digital camera.
2. Provide participants with a set of clear guidelines (e.g., take photographs of out-of-class language learning).
3. Provide participants with technological support.

Audio/Video Recording

1. If possible, provide participants with access to an audio/video recorder.
2. Provide participants with a set of clear guidelines (e.g., describe your out-of-class language learning).
3. Provide technical support for sound and/or visual editing.

Digital Narratives

Most students will find it more comfortable to write their LLHs or narratives using word processing software before transferring the content to an online platform (e.g., blog and website).

1. Provide participants with a set of instructions as well as guidelines for how to include multimodal components (e.g., photographs, graphics, comics, video).
2. Help participants to map out the insertion and position of non-textual components.
3. Provide technical support for content transfer and/or integration or uploading of multimedia components.

Data Management

1. Digitize non-digital photographs (e.g., taken from a disposable camera) because photographs can fade quite quickly.
2. Download audio or video files.
3. Use the archive function on websites to save and store webpages, if available. Availability depends on the type of account (free or premium). An alternative is screen-capturing the display of a website. The advantage is the freedom from account restrictions, but the downside is the loss of interactivity included in the original texts.

4.5 Conclusion

This chapter has presented three examples of producing and using multimedia narrative data, including photographs, digital LLHs, and online LLHs. The first part of the chapter outlined various contexts in which such narratives are produced or elicited for the purposes of inquiry. The three featured studies illustrate the narrative data types and uses. In each case the data collection process has been described in detail in the hope that this serves an instructive purpose for readers. We concluded the chapter with a brief discussion of some of the ethical issues specifically related to the elicitation, use, and archiving of multimedia narrative data.

5

DATA ANALYSIS IN NARRATIVE INQUIRY

5.1 Introduction

5.1.1 Narrative Inquiry and Qualitative Research

Because narrative inquiry is a form of qualitative research, narrative studies often employ the same approaches to data analysis that are used in other types of qualitative research. Much of what we have to say about these approaches, therefore, is covered in detail in books on qualitative research methodology. In this chapter we discuss these qualitative approaches briefly and then turn to approaches that are specific to narrative inquiry. We begin with a brief discussion of three key terms—"iterative," "emergent," and "interpretive"—as they are used in Dörnyei's (2007) chapter on qualitative research in order to establish a broad framework for the data analysis strategies outlined later.

Iterative: Dörnyei (2007: 243) contrasts the "orderly" patterns of quantitative research, where there is a clear break between data collection and data analysis, with the iterative, or "zigzag," patterns of qualitative research, where researchers often "move back and forth between data collection, data analysis and data interpretation." Iterative data analysis stops at the point of "saturation," when further data collection, analysis, or interpretation is unlikely to yield additional insight or, more practically, when a piece of work needs to be completed and written up.

Emergent: Iteration implies an emergent research design, in which "a study is kept open and fluid so that it can respond in a flexible way to new details or openings" (Dörnyei, 2007: 37). This often means that research findings are teased out during repeated rounds of data analysis. Qualitative research may also begin with open-ended aims and objectives, so that research questions, as well as the answers to them, may emerge during data analysis.

Interpretive: Qualitative research is "fundamentally interpretive," in the sense that the research outcome is ultimately the product of the researcher's subjective interpretation of the data" (Dörnyei, 2007: 37). When researchers write that findings "emerged," it sometimes seems as if they climbed out of the data by themselves! In fact, findings only emerge as a result of hard, and often creative, interpretive work by the researchers.

Bearing in mind that narrative inquiry is a form of qualitative research, we encourage readers to keep these three terms firmly in mind while reading this chapter. By discussing data collection and data analysis in separate chapters of this book, we do not mean to suggest that they are separate processes in narrative inquiry. Data analysis can begin at any point in a study and an early start is often advisable because preliminary analyses may help refine data collection strategies. Data analysis strategies are also best applied with the words "iterative," "emergent," and "interpretive" in mind. In many narrative studies, the basic approach is to read, discuss, and write about the data repeatedly and with an open mind. More specific strategies help make this basic approach more relevant to the form of the data than it might otherwise be. They also make data analysis more systematic or rigorous. They are intended, however, to aid, not replace, subjective interpretation.

5.1.2 Narrative and Non-narrative Data

Despite what we have said about iteration in qualitative research design, it is often a good idea to identify a point in a study at which data collection is provisionally complete and some formal process of data analysis that will lead to the publication of research findings begins. Let us assume that we have reached this point and that we have a package of data ready for analysis. The first thing to consider is the form of the data. In earlier chapters we have discussed spoken, written, or multimodal data collection. We now assume that we have this data in hand and ask whether it is "narrative" or "non-narrative"' in form. By "narrative" we mean that data is already in story form; it consists, for example, of published language learning memoirs, elicited language learning histories (LLHs), or completed narrative frames. By "non-narrative" we mean that the data is not yet in story form; it consists, for example, of interview transcripts, diaries or reflective journals, multimodal texts, or the various sources that often make up ethnographic data sets.

The significance of this distinction lies in what happens next. Will the data analysis be a matter of analyzing one or more narratives or will it be a matter of using narrative writing as a strategy to analyze non-narrative data? Polkinghorne (1995) describes two kinds of narrative inquiry studies, involving (a) "analysis of narratives" ("studies whose data consist of narratives or stories, but whose analysis produces paradigmatic typologies or categories") and (b) "narrative analysis" ("studies whose data consist of actions, events, and happenings, but whose analysis produces stories") (pp. 5–6). The distinction between narrative and non-narrative data is fuzzy, however, and often comes down to how researchers choose to look at their data. We have described interviews, for example, as non-narrative data, but they are also treated as sources of narrative data in language teaching and learning research in three ways:

1. If the interview is designed to elicit a story (e.g., an interviewee's language learning history), the interviewee's contribution to the story may be treated as a narrative.
2. The researcher may produce an edited narrative summary of the interviewee's contribution for further analysis.
3. The researcher may select for analysis a short extract from an interview in which the interviewee tells a story.

There is, therefore, no hard and fast rule for deciding whether data is narrative or non-narrative in form. It is important to decide how you intend to approach your data, however, because the narrative/non-narrative distinction points to different paths for data analysis.

Polkinghorne's distinction is fundamental to the organization of this chapter, although we discuss three, rather than two, broad approaches to data analysis. Under the heading "analyzing narrative data" (i.e., "analysis of narratives"), we discuss two approaches: one based on thematic analysis of the content of narratives (5.2), which Polkinghorne treats in some detail, and the other based on discourse analysis of the structure and language of narratives (5.3), to which he pays less attention. Under the heading "narrative writing" (i.e., "narrative analysis") we discuss the third approach, how storytelling can be used as a data analysis strategy (5.4). This chapter concludes with a discussion of the nature of findings in narrative inquiry that will lead us into considerations of rigor, trustworthiness, and generalizability, which are, in part, ethical (5.5).

5.2 Analyzing Narrative Data: Thematic Analysis

Referring to Bruner's (1986) distinction between narrative and paradigmatic modes of thought, Polkinghorne (1995) uses the term "paradigmatic" to describe the characteristic mode of analysis of narrative data. Paradigmatic analysis is largely a matter of categorization and classification, in which particular instances of phenomena are linked to more general concepts. It also involves the use of abstract reasoning to establish theoretical relationships between concepts derived from the data. In qualitative research, the approach is called "thematic," "content," or "grounded theory" analysis, although the latter term may be best reserved for work that draws directly on the work of Glaser and Strauss (1967). Because thematic analysis is discussed in detail in qualitative data analysis manuals (e.g., Bogdan and Biklen, 2006; Corbin and Strauss, 2008; Miles and Huberman, 1994; Richards,

2003; Silverman, 2006), we will describe it only briefly here. In general terms, it involves repeated reading of the data, coding and categorization of data extracts, and their reorganization under thematic headings. In published narrative studies major themes are typically discussed in separate sections of the report, where they are broken down into subthemes and illustrated by extracts from the narratives.

Polkinghorne identifies paradigmatic analysis with analysis of the "content" of narratives or *what* they say about their subject matter. As we will see in the next section (5.3), a similar approach has been applied to the discourse of narratives, or *how* they say what they say about their subject matter. In this section, we focus on thematic analysis of content, using our first featured study (Gao, 2010) as an example of thematic analysis of narratives produced by a single individual (5.2.1). Later, we will look at issues that arise in the more typical application of thematic analysis in multiple case studies (5.2.2).

5.2.1 Thematic Analysis: Single Case Studies

BOX 5.1

> Observing that language learners' stories are often bestsellers in Asia, Gao (2010) investigated published autobiographical narratives written by Zhang Haidi, a paraplegic language learner, in China. Although unable to attend school, Zhang reached a level in English where she was able to translate books into Chinese and offer advice to other learners. Gao's sources of data included her autobiography and extracts from her diaries and letters. His aim was to explore the reasons for her success in terms of characteristics of autonomous learning.
>
> Gao describes his data analysis as "paradigmatic" (Polkinghorne, 1995) and explains that extracts from the narratives were first selected and categorized according to three themes that have been identified as important to autonomous learning in the literature: motivational discourses, language learning beliefs, and strategic learning efforts. Gao coded and reconstructed the narratives under these themes and in the findings section of the paper each theme is developed and illustrated by short extracts from Zhang's narratives. Each theme is divided into subthemes. Under learning beliefs, for example, Gao identifies two subthemes concerned with memorization and language use.
>
> Gao concludes that Zhang's narratives confirm the importance of motivational discourses, language learning beliefs, and strategic learning efforts in autonomous language learning. He also shows how these factors were shaped both by the contextual conditions of Zhang's restricted physical mobility and the social and political discourses of post-Cultural Revolution China, and by Zhang's strong sense of agency.

Gao (2010) exemplifies the use of thematic analysis in the context of a study of published narratives written by a disabled Chinese language learner. Gao describes the analysis as "paradigmatic" and his overall aim is to produce an argument on the importance of certain factors in autonomous learning and to support it with evidence from the narratives. A distinction is sometimes made between strategies in which themes are determined in advance and strategies in which they are allowed to emerge as the analysis proceeds. Gao (2010) clearly adopts the first strategy. His three major themes—motivation, beliefs, and strategies—come from a review of literature on autonomous learning and not from the analysis itself. These themes were built into his research questions from the outset and the analysis of the narratives involved a search for evidence related to them.

Analyzing autobiographical accounts of her own learning and teaching of English, Sakui adopts the second approach, which is often identified with "grounded theory" (as opposed to "content analysis"):

> Adopting the Grounded Theory analysis method, I first coded these data and sources inductively. Semantic coding was carried out at several levels . . . After I obtained a list of codings, I categorized them into larger themes. Finally, these themes were examined and compared for their interrelationships. (2002: 138, see Chapter 3)

Sakui's approach is more open-ended than Gao's and in each case the choice of approach is justified by the researcher's objectives. Gao (2010), for example, wanted to explore what an analysis of Zhang's narratives would add to our understanding of established theory in the literature on autonomous learning. Sakui (2002), on the other hand, wanted to explore relationships between teaching and earlier experiences of learning—an area in which there was little established theory. This is reflected in the themes under which she organizes her findings: her competencies and limitations, beliefs and practices, and relationships between herself and her teaching. Whether themes are determined in advance or not, good thematic analysis always involves repeated reading of the data and several rounds of analysis, in which the researcher moves back and forth between the data and its coded and categorized forms in order to refine themes and theoretical relationships.

One of the risks involved in content analysis, however, is that we will simply look for occasions on which pre-determined themes are explicitly mentioned in the narratives and fail to dig more deeply into the data. Gao (2010) reduced this risk by paying close attention to the meaning of data extracts, which led to the emergence of subthemes that were not pre-determined. Analyzing Zhang's use of learning strategies, for example, he left the question of which strategies were important in autonomous learning open. He also interpreted certain data extracts as providing evidence of strategy preferences even when the strategy was not explicitly mentioned. For example, he interprets the following extract from a letter as evidence of the importance of memorization as a strategy:

If the foundation is not solid, there will be no significant progress. Just like verb tenses, the use of prepositions and so on, we have to master them. (Gao, 2010: 585)

In the same letter, Zhang advises her reader to "eat" more books by "repeatedly reading, understanding and digesting them word by word, sentence by sentence." This also illustrates how larger themes are interpretively built up from smaller themes. In this case, Gao builds up the subtheme of "memorization" (under the theme of strategy use) from references to a "solid foundation," "mastery," "repeated reading," and so on. These are good examples of how researchers connect particular instances to more general concepts as they code and categorize their data.

Cotterall's (2004, see Chapter 2) longitudinal narrative study of an Australian university student's participation in a Spanish course illustrates an approach to thematic analysis that lies between Gao's and Sakui's approaches. Cotterall explains that although the themes she identified were not predetermined, they were related to a broad theoretical agenda concerned with learners' goals and beliefs about language learning and control of the learning process. The themes that emerged were "the gradual narrowing of the learner's goals, the learner's fluctuating affective state and his changing conceptions of the nature of language learning" (pp. 106–7). Cotterall also tried to avoid a further risk in thematic analysis of narrative data: the loss of the sequential coherence of the narrative in the process of coding, categorization, and re-organization of extracts. By discussing data extracts under each heading in the chronological order they were produced, she attempted to capture the important dimension of changes in the student's perceptions over time (see also Casanave, 2012, and Chapter 6.5).

5.2.2 Thematic Analysis: Multiple Case Studies

The three examples of thematic analysis that we have discussed so far are individual case studies. However, thematic analysis is more frequently employed in studies involving multiple participants and multiple narratives. Indeed, thematic analysis is probably best suited to multiple case studies, because it opens up the possibility of comparing the narratives in a data set, of establishing shared themes, as well as highlighting individual differences. Polkinghorne (1995: 15), for example, argues that the "strength of paradigmatic procedures is their capacity to develop general knowledge about a collection of stories." The number of participants in multiple narrative studies can vary greatly, and in the studies that we include in this section, the numbers vary from two to more than 100. The second featured study in this section (Chik, 2011), therefore, lies in the mid-range as a study of ten LLHs. The innovative way in which these ten narratives are brought together in Chik's study highlights how the relationships in which the researcher places the narratives in a database is a crucial element in data analysis.

Beginning with studies that involve fewer participants and narratives, we note that two is the minimum number for a multiple case study and that in several published studies two narratives are selected from a larger set, in order to highlight a contrast of some kind. In her study of the narratives of Latin American adults enrolled in an ESL program in California, Menard-Warwick (2004) used an open-coding approach to examine learners' gender-mediated decisions about learning English. The published report focused on two of the eight participants, who were selected because they took the most strongly contrasting positions on gender issues. By contrasting these narratives, she found that gender identities were a key factor in learners' decisions, but that individuals "interpreted the cultural imperatives of gender in varied ways, depending on their histories and present circumstances" (p. 295).

Gao, Li, and Li (2002) used open coding of three narratives to highlight the role of individual agency in the construction of Chinese college English majors' learning environments and self-identities. The main themes identified were (1) pre-college language-learning orientation, (2) interaction between college input and personal effort, (3) identity conflicts, (4) future direction of development, and (5) a stable 'core identity' or identities. In this study, comparison was used not to contrast different positions, but to demonstrate diversity in the relationship between English language learning and identity construction among the participants. These themes identified were helpful in this respect, because they provided a structure in which to explore differences among the three participants' narratives.

Another approach to analyzing a small number of narratives from participants who are judged to share certain social and psychological experiences is to combine elements from the narratives into a single, collective "metanarrative." Coryell, Clark, and Pomerantz (2010, see Chapter 2), for example, drew on narratives produced during interviews by adult learners of Spanish as a heritage language in the United States to produce what they call a "cultural fantasy metanarrative." In order to do this, they used the words and phrases that the participants used to talk about "proper Spanish" and "Tex-Mex" to code narrative data related to their opinions about varieties of Spanish and develop subthemes through which the women made sense of their identities. Nekvapil (2003) discusses a similar approach to the construction of the "typical" language biography of German speakers in post-war Czechoslovakia, which, he argues, incorporates both individual and "collective historical features" due both to shared experience and "the fact that the informants are likely to resume in their narratives the narratives they have heard from different sources during their lives" (p. 75).

BOX 5.2

Chik's (2011) study is based on an analysis of ten LLHs, written up as summaries of interview data during her doctoral research. The participants were Hong Kong students in five different age groups, who began learning English as a second language in kindergarten. The research design was "longitudinal" in that each participant was interviewed three times over a period of two and a half years. The design was also "cross-sectional" in that developments over time were inferred from comparison of students in different age groups. In this way, she was able to observe continuous developments across overlapping age ranges from 8–10 to 18–20 years old.

The study is a re-analysis of the LLHs from the perspective of language awareness. The focus of the paper is the development of language awareness among students who begin learning English in school from an early age. Chik describes her method of analyzing the LLHs as "focused reading" and "content analysis" leading to the emergence of themes concerned with conceptions of English: "English as an academic subject," "English as a language system," and English use in contexts of "competition" and "communication."

In the findings section of the paper, these themes are ordered so as to represent the development across the age range of the participants. Chik concludes that language awareness first involves the learners' awareness of themselves as individuals learning a foreign language in a specific socio-cultural-educational context and that it develops through the expansion of their social worlds.

Where the number of narratives is relatively small, therefore, there are three basic options for comparative thematic analysis: to analyze each narrative individually and treat them as either contrasting or diverse cases; or to analyze them collectively and treat them as aspects of a single, collective case. The featured study in this section (Chik, 2011) offers an innovative approach to combining narratives in a study based on ten LLHs. Chik wrote up histories based on interviews with two students (one male, one female) in five different age groups over a period of two and a half years. She then "chained" the histories together to make one continuous history, from which she inferred typical developments in a Hong Kong student's language learning from age 8 to 20. By including two students in each age group, she was able to allow for variations in individual experience.

In the case of LLH and narrative frame studies, the number of cases is usually so large as to preclude individual analysis and the tendency is to aggregate the data and search for themes that run across the data set as a whole. Murphey, Chen, and Chen (2004, see Chapter 3) draw on 142 short LLHs written by Japanese and Taiwanese university students. The researchers report that the narratives were "consistently irregular" and did "not allow for a neat quantitative analysis," but that there were "patterns connecting the histories together" concerned with identity and imagined communities (p. 83). In the published report, excerpts from the narratives are quoted and discussed under headings related to "degrees of identification or non-identification and investment with imagined communities" (p. 86). In this study, it seems that the data were not analyzed systematically, but were instead "mined" for examples that would illustrate a more impressionistic theoretical analysis. Yelenevskaya and Fialkova (2003) use a similar strategy in their paper on multilingualism and language awareness based on 115 narrative interviews with Israeli immigrants from the former Soviet Union. The researchers describe their analytical approach as "content analysis," but their discussion of data is organized around a selection of extracts from the interviews that are accompanied by analytical commentaries highlighting different themes. This paper also provides an interesting example of iteration in data collection and analysis, as an analysis of the first twenty interviews led to the addition of themes to later interviews.

While large narrative data sets are often treated as "mines" or "pools" of data for relatively unsystematic exploration, more systematic approaches are also found. Takeuchi (2003), for example, examined sixty-seven books written by successful foreign language learners and published in Japan. He systematically identified and categorized each mention of learning strategy use and correlated them with the stage of learning (beginner, intermediate, and advanced). Some of the texts were also coded by a second researcher. Murphey and Carpenter (2008) also used a more systematic approach to an analysis of twenty university students' LLHs, in which extracts were coded for "factors that learners reported as useful, helpful, or encouraging, and instances in which learner agency was evident" (p. 22). Extracts were also coded for the phase of education, positive or negative influence, and learning context. This led to quantitative correlation analysis of codes for 568 extracts. While Murphey and Carpenter's study is unusual among narrative studies of language teaching and learning, it raises interesting questions about the degree to which analysis of narrative corpora can and should be systematically carried out.

Narrative frames are also designed to collect short narratives in relatively large quantities, and studies published to date have followed Barkhuizen and Wette (2008: 376, see Chapter 3) in using a "qualitative content analysis" approach, in which "themes were coded and categorized, patterns in the themes were identified and during this process interpretations of the themes were made" (see also Barnard and Nguyen, 2010; Macalister, 2012; Wette and Barkhuizen, 2009). Wette and Barkhuizen also explain that the data were organized so that they could retrieve each teacher's profile of twenty-nine responses, while each response was coded separately using N-Vivo qualitative data analysis software so that interpretations could be made across the database. In this study, they report that "coding categories were generated inductively from analysis of the data as well as from themes identified in the literature . . . a process that narrative frames greatly assisted" (p. 201).

As we noted earlier, thematic analysis is essentially a qualitative approach to analyzing narrative data. It is an effective way of linking data extracts to more abstract categories and concepts and of re-arranging them in support of theoretical arguments. It is helpful in identifying points of similarity and difference across narratives and, if applied rigorously, it can ensure that the researcher pays attention to all of the data using the same analytical lens. This strength can also be seen as a weakness, however, in that there is inevitably a degree to which the narrative character of the data is lost in the process of analysis. As Polkinghorne (1995: 15) argues, thematic procedures have the "capacity to develop general knowledge about a collection of stories," but the knowledge that is produced is "abstract and formal, and by necessity underplays the unique and particular aspects of each story." He makes this point in the context of an argument that "narrative analysis," or narrative writing as a method of analysis, could be more widely used in narrative inquiry. Before we turn to narrative writing as a strategy for language teaching and learning research, however, we will consider a third approach that involves addressing the content of narrative through discourse analysis.

5.3 Analyzing Narrative Discourse

Under the heading of paradigmatic analysis, Polkinghorne (1995: 14) briefly mentions studies that focus on what he calls the "formal attributes of storied narratives," but he does so only briefly because they do not address the "content and meaning" of data, which are of primary interest to qualitative researchers. The kinds of studies that he has in mind are those such as Propp's (1968) analysis of the "morphology" of fairy tales, which tells us a great deal about fairy tales as narratives, but little about their content or meaning. More recently, however, a body of work has begun to emerge that is interested in what narratives reveal about discursively constructed experience. In these studies the content and meaning of experience are treated as products of narrative discourse that can be investigated through the study of the structure, language, and uses of narratives (see, for example, Ochs and Capps, 2001; Thornborrow and Coates, 2005). Gao (2010: 528) provides an example of this approach in the context of a largely thematic analysis, when he acknowledges the risk of treating his data extracts as "factual representations." He also comments on the different ways in which Zhang Haidi represented her motivation in earlier texts published by the Communist Youth League, which highlighted the role of socialist ideals, and in her later autobiography, published in a changed political climate, which put more emphasis on visions of her "ideal self." In this section we look at several strategies that explore language learning and teaching experiences by looking both "at" and "through" narrative data (Bailey, 1983).

5.3.1 Metaphors

One strategy that has been used in several studies relies on identification and interpretation of metaphors (O'Sullivan, 2010; Oxford, 2001). Oxford (2001) analyzed 120 short written narratives in which students talked about teachers. Oxford explains how, interested in conflicts between teachers' instructional styles and students' learning styles, she began by using "content analysis," but shifted to a grounded theory approach based on coding explicit and implicit metaphors. The categories that she came up with included, for example, the teacher as "hanging judge," "nurturer/inspirer," "role model," and "witch." These metaphors were subsequently analyzed in relation to the cultural background of the writers and a theoretical model of teaching approaches. O'Sullivan (2010) used metaphor as an analytical device to examine representations of relationships between non-native and native speakers in published language learning memoirs and came up with five main metaphors that are discussed as themes in the paper: the foreign language as a "human being," the non-native/non-fluent speaker as a "child," the foreign language and culture as a "trap," the foreign language as a "costume," and the foreign culture as a "play." In both cases, the approach involves a kind of "content analysis," but the target is a specific linguistic feature, rather than a construct or idea.

5.3.2 Narrative Structure

A second strategy has been to pay attention to structural features of narratives. Menezes (2008, see Chapter 4), for example, examined how learners constructed openings and closings of multimodal LLHs and how different elements—"family, cultural history, educational artefacts (book, dictionaries), school teachers, classmates, etc." (p. 206)—are related to each other in terms of dynamic non-linear processes in their narratives. She concluded that second language knowledge is not only "a product of formal learning contexts, but it emerges out of the interaction of different social networks (family, cultural production, school) with the individual cognitive and affective factors" (p. 213). This conclusion is based on both the content and discourse of the narratives—on what the learners say, but more importantly how they organize what they say.

Investigating "the construction of the language-learning experience" in autobiographical accounts of adults in the United Kingdom who had learned French, Coffey (2010) divided the accounts into storied episodes, which were analyzed according to the "interpretive repertoires" that the narrators used to refer to French, France, and the French. In particular, he focused on how the narrators integrated images of France and Frenchness into their accounts by "constructing points of sameness and difference that were expressed as temporal and spatial 'turning points'" (p. 125). In conclusion, Coffey identified two main "narrative positions" underlying the desire to learn French: (1) Frenchness as an aesthetic ideal (a shared cultural repertoire of otherness), and (2) France as a place of encounter (an individual repertoire of personal transformation).

In both of these studies there is, in fact, a clear focus on the identification of themes—for Menezes (2008) the people and objects involved in language learning, for Coffey (2010) the ideas of France and French. But in contrast to the thematic strategies discussed earlier, in which themes tend to be removed from the specific narrative contexts in which they naturally occur for further analysis, in Menezes's and Coffey's work conclusions depend upon the ways in which their themes are articulated as structural elements of the narratives they investigate.

5.3.3 Narrative in Interaction

A third strategy based on narrative discourse focuses on narrative in interaction and differs from other approaches in dealing exclusively with short narratives that occur in natural spoken interaction. Its use in language teaching and learning research has been influenced by the idea of "small stories" (Bamberg, 2006; Watson, 2007) and, in particular, by an analytical approach involving "positioning analysis," outlined and illustrated in Bamberg and Georgakopoulou (2008). Positioning analysis has been used in several recent language teaching and learning studies, including the featured study in this section (Barkhuizen, 2010; see also Rugen, 2010; Simpson, 2011; Vásquez, 2011).

For Watson (2007: 371) the difference between "big stories" and "small stories" is the difference between "the big retrospectives elicited from interviews" and the "ephemeral narratives emerging in everyday mundane contexts." Bamberg (2006), who was the first to develop this contrast in the context of research on identity, argues that the problem with "big stories" is that "when we are discussing narratives, we are neither accessing speakers' past experiences nor their reflections on their past experiences" (p. 144). Small story research, therefore, involves a critique of so-called "big story" research that we will return to later (5.5). To date, "positioning analysis" (Davies and Harré, 1990) has been the primary data analysis strategy in small story research, a discourse analysis strategy that involves identification and interpretation of the interactional features through which speakers identify self and others in terms of mutual relationships in interaction and relationships to wider contexts of discourse.

BOX 5.3

Barkhuizen (2010) analyzes a "small story" told by Sela, a Tongan pre-service English teacher in New Zealand, during a research interview. Barkhuizen is interested in how Sela talks about her identity in the story and in order to learn more about this he uses what he calls an "extended version" of the "positioning analysis" approach to narrative data analysis outlined by Bamberg and Georgakopoulou (2008).

Barkhuizen conducted three rounds of data analysis, focusing first on the content and characters in Sela's story, then on the interactive performance of the story during the interview, and lastly on the positions that Sela adopted in relation to normative discourses of immigration. Barkhuizen then "extended" the analysis by drawing on Sela's "bigger story," or what he can infer from other data that he collected from her.

The overall aim of the analysis is to understand how Sela addresses the question, "Who am I?", which Barkhuizen discusses under the headings, "Tongan migrant," "Teacher," "Activist/mediator," and "Investor/capitalizer." Barkhuizen concludes that her story reveals "how she has positioned herself as complicit with a dominant ELT ideology, expressed particularly as an economic metaphor of investment, capitalization and a better life" (p. 296).

While Barkhuizen (2010) analyzes a narrative extract from a research interview, Simpson (2011) focuses on a stretch of "narrative-in-interaction" from a classroom discussion between the researcher and an adult migrant ESOL student in the United Kingdom. In both cases, the data consists of a short extract from the transcription, which is included in the paper as an appendix. Both researchers adopt a three-step analytical procedure based on three "positioning levels": (1) how the characters in the story are positioned in relation to each other, (2) how the speakers position themselves in relation to each other, and (3) how speakers construct themselves and others in terms of teller roles and "dominant discourses or master narratives" (Bamberg and Georgakopoulou, 2008: 385). In Simpson's paper, positioning analysis reveals how ESOL classroom discourse constrains the identity positions made available to migrant students and how one student resists this positioning. While Simpson accepts the self-imposed constraint in the small story approach of relying only on the small story, Barkhuizen (2010) "extends" the approach by drawing on other sources of data (research interviews and reflective journals).

5.4 Narrative Writing

By "narrative analysis," Polkinghorne (1995) means an approach to the analysis of varied data sources that is based on the construction of narratives. In thematic analysis of narratives, categorization and the construction of theoretical relationships among abstract categories are the main analytical tools. In narrative analysis, narrative itself becomes an analytical tool that is brought to bear through "narrative writing." The outcomes of narrative writing in narrative inquiry include historical accounts, case studies, or storied episodes of people's lives. For Polkinghorne (1995: 5), the narrative that is produced "gives meaning to the data as contributors to a goal or purpose" and the key narrative device is "a plot that displays the linkage among the data elements as parts of an unfolding temporal development culminating in the denouement." The plot of a narrative account corresponds to the relationships of causality that are central to paradigmatic accounts. The plot of the narrative explains whatever it is that the researcher seeks to explain within a particular context of experience.

BOX 5.4

O'Móchain (2006) is a narrative account of an English as a Foreign Language course taught by the author. The setting was a content-based English course on Cultural Studies at a Christian two-year women's college in Japan. O'Móchain describes the college environment as strongly heteronormative. His aim in the course was to find "a context-appropriate way of exploring gender and sexuality issues" and, in particular, to develop "a teaching strategy that would focus on queer lives in the local context" (p. 51).

Narrative appears in the paper at three levels. First, O'Móchain used life history interviews with local gay-identified individuals as teaching materials for the course and students were also encouraged to tell stories in discussion. Second, these narrative materials are summarized in the paper together with a student's story about a transgender schoolmate. Lastly, the paper itself is constructed as a narrative; the literature review takes the form of a narrative of the author's reading and is followed by a narrative account of his experience of teaching the course interspersed with the narrative materials from the course itself.

O'Móchain concludes that the teaching strategy was effective in that several students "showed a readiness to challenge the dominance of heteronormative paradigms" and that "a queer narrative approach may prove valuable in providing much-needed affirmation for queer-identifying students, as well as promoting empathetic values and open-ended imaginations of gender and sexuality for all students" (p. 64).

The featured study in this section (O'Móchain, 2006) is a good example of a study in which narrative writing is used as an analytical strategy. O'Móchain does not describe the data collection or analysis procedures and it is clear that they were relatively informal. The data that appear in the paper include the author's recollections, course materials, and audio-recordings of classroom discussions, and the analysis was evidently no more than a matter of crafting a story based on these materials. Papers of this kind often struggle to find a place in academic journals. Reviewers often do not consider them to be "research," because they lack the formal data collection and analysis procedures found in papers based on paradigmatic methods. It is worth reflecting, therefore, on the qualities of papers such as O'Móchain's that make them count as "research" from the perspective of narrative inquiry.

In the first instance, O'Móchain's paper is not simply a story about a course that he taught. It is a story about a course that addresses an issue of importance to the field of language teaching and learning research: how to address questions of gender and sexual diversity in language teaching in culturally sensitive ways in environments that appear hostile to the idea of diversity itself. This focus on an issue of importance relates to what is often called the "tellability" of a story. Second, the paper has a strong plotline that takes the reader through the author's planning of the course based on his reading and understanding of the setting, the implementation of the course, and the occurrence of certain unexpected events. Most importantly, O'Móchain draws on relevant detail to create a plot that is both compelling and explanatory. The story that he tells does not lead to any abstract or generalizable theoretical point, but it does leave the reader with a clear understanding of how the course addressed the issue that it was designed to address in the particular context in which the researcher works.

O'Móchain's paper is autobiographical in that it focuses on the author's own experiences. In this respect it is similar to Campbell's (1996) diary study (see Chapter 3), in which there is a detailed description of the data collection, but no description of the analysis that leads to the published findings. However, the paper has the clear aim of explaining how Campbell's strategy use during a Spanish course in Mexico was influenced by an earlier experience of learning German in Germany. Campbell achieves this aim largely through a compelling and artfully constructed narrative account.

Fries's article (1998) is a recollective account of her long-term experiences of bilingualism as a non-native speaker of French in France, in which there is no explicit mention of data collection or analysis. In this case, however, there is a clear sense in which the construction of the narrative involves a filtering and reorganization of a mass of experience to achieve a narrative focus. Her report is not simply an account of the author's life as a bilingual in France, but a highly selective account of language-related experiences that provides deep insight into the more general experience of long-term bilingualism. Distance and reflectivity are also important qualities of these autobiographical accounts, in which the authors succeed in examining their inner worlds of language learning and use, and writing about them, as it were, from the outside.

Narrative writing is also used as a data analysis strategy in biographical, or third-person case studies, by Chik and Benson (2008) and Xu and Liu (2009, see both Chapter 2). In these studies, the approach to narrative writing is explicitly stated. Chik and Benson include the following description of their procedure of analyzing interviews conducted over a four-year period with a Hong Kong student who studied in the United Kingdom:

> After transcription, the first two interviews were coded thematically, with Ally's language background and her expectations and evaluations of overseas study emerging as important themes and the clash between

her expectations prior to departure and evaluations after two years overseas emerging as a key to the narrative structure of her experience. Using
short narratives of critical incidents within the data as core elements, Ally's
experiences were written up in story form. Ally then read this story and
commented on it during the third interview. This interview was also coded,
with the themes of re-evaluation and awareness of identity change emerging strongly. A summary of this interview was used as a concluding section
to the narrative. (2008: 158–9)

This description explains how the clash between expectations and evaluations of
study abroad provided a central theme for a narrative that provides insight into the
dynamic and contextual character of language learning identities as they develop
over time.

We noted how narrative appears at several levels in O'Móchain's (2006) paper
and this is also a feature of papers by Xu and Liu (2009) and Liu and Xu (2011).
Their approach draws on Clandinin and Connelly's (2000) view of narrative
inquiry as involving narrative both as a "social phenomenon (storied experience)"
and as a "method of data analysis (restorying)" (Liu and Xu, 2011: 591). In their
research, this involves working with Mainland Chinese teachers' stories through
a process of interaction with the researchers that encourages the teachers to "tell
and retell, live and relive the stories" (Clandinin and Connelly, 2000). Both studies
are built around three short stories originally told by a single case study participant. In a study focusing on one teacher's experiences of educational reform and
based on interviews, written reflection reports, and reflective journals, Liu and
Xu (2011: 591) describe their four-step data analysis procedure in some detail
under the headings: (1) making sense of the narratives, (2) coding for themes,
(3) reconstructing the narratives for a storyline, and (4) telling and retelling, living
and reliving the stories. This process led to the writing of the three stories that are
reported in the paper together with the researchers' interpretation of them.

Another approach to third-person narrative analysis is found in Shedivy's
(2004) study of factors that lead some students to persist in foreign language
learning beyond school. She describes a four-step phenomenological approach
to analysis of interview transcripts: (1) reading the transcripts in their entirety,
(2) extracting significant statements from each transcript, (3) formulating statements into meanings, and clustering these meanings into themes, (4) integrating
themes into narrative descriptions. Although this approach appears to be similar
to thematic approaches, the important difference is that the data are not coded,
but reduced to condensed statements of meaning, which can later be used to
reconstitute a narrative. The problem addressed here is how to reduce the long
and possibly incoherent text of an interview transcript to a shorter, coherent narrative that brings out the meaning of a phenomenon for the participant. Kvale and
Brinkmann (2009: 205) use the term "meaning condensation" to describe a similar analytical procedure, whereby "long statements are compressed into briefer

statements in which the main sense of what is said is rephrased in a few words." Shedivy (2004: 108) also refers to the importance of distance in retelling the participants' stories. Commenting on her own prior belief in the importance of integrative motivation to persistence, she comments that she had to "set aside and monitor" her belief that "there was some sort of integrative switch that students could turn on." As she did not find this switch, she had to seek alternative explanations for persistence in the data.

5.5 Findings in Narrative Inquiry

In conventional research terminology, the outcomes of data analysis are "findings," which often take the form of statements representing the contribution of the research to knowledge of the topic investigated. This contribution may take several forms: for example, a simple addition to or a more complex revision of what we know, leading to new problems or questions. In quantitative research, procedures for generating and evaluating findings are formalized: for example, hypotheses are tested using validated research instruments and results are evaluated using statistical procedures. "Findings" are, in effect, statements backed up by evidence of statistical significance. The formality of these procedures lends a degree of "objectivity" to the findings of quantitative research. This does not necessarily mean that they have the status of "fact," but rather that they are produced through procedures that conform to conventionalized standards.

The findings of narrative inquiry studies, and qualitative studies more generally, are never "objective" in this sense and there is, indeed, often an explicit acknowledgement that they are necessarily "subjective" and "interpretive." By this we mean that there are always moments in data analysis where the precise processes of analysis can only be described with great difficulty, if at all. These are often moments of insight or intuition, at which the researchers bring their subjective knowledge and cognitive capacities to bear on the data in ways that only become apparent through their outcomes. A quantitative study is judged to be "reliable," when the data collection and analysis are carried out in such a way that their replication would produce the same results. The notion of "reliability" makes little sense in narrative inquiry, because of the multiple levels at which individuality and uniqueness are at issue: in participants' experiences, their stories, the telling of their stories, and their interpretation and retelling of these stories in the context of a research report. Narrative studies can never be replicable, because they are always products of unique interpretations of unique sets of data. This also implies that their findings are ultimately the product of the researchers' subjectivity: something that the researchers have to say about a particular set of data that they have collected.

In qualitative research this is, perhaps, a matter of degree that is reflected in the different approaches to data analysis in narrative inquiry that we have discussed in this chapter. It would be absurd, for example, to think of a paper such as O'Móchain's (2006), in which the outcome is a narrative written by the researcher, as being in any way replicable. Yet it would not be absurd at all to ask whether, in papers that use thematic or discourse approaches to the analysis of narrative data (e.g., Gao, 2010; Barkhuizen, 2010; Chik, 2011), the analysis would be enhanced by a second coding of the data to ensure inter-rater reliability. We may also ask, however, whether such procedures really belong to narrative research, in which we are not looking for "objective" or "reliable" findings, but for a well-crafted, subjective interpretation of data, whether it comes in the form of a paradigmatic argument based on thematic or discourse analysis or in the form of a narrative written by the researcher. Within this understanding, researchers, nevertheless, need to pay attention to three important issues concerned with both the quality and ethics of data analysis, which we discuss under the heading of rigor, trustworthiness, and the generalizability of findings.

5.5.1 Rigor

By "rigor" we mean the degree to which an analysis is systematic with regard to both the coverage of data and the application of analytical procedures. There is a general expectation in research that data analysis should be thoroughgoing. This means, in principle, that all the available data should be analyzed and that data analysis procedures should be applied systematically. In narrative inquiry, this is often achieved through the thematic and discourse analysis procedures discussed in this chapter, which typically prescribe that the data is systematically searched for the occurrence of a particular theme or discourse, or that the data is read and coded repeatedly. In published reports, the degree of rigor in the data analysis is often articulated in the methodology section. Barkhuizen (2010) is an example of a paper that includes an explicit and detailed account of the data analysis procedures. By providing only a cursory account of the data analysis or no account at all, researchers can give an impression that the analysis was less rigorous than it might have been.

Rigor in narrative writing is less easily demonstrated, although an expectation that the researchers attend to all of their data sources and account for the main steps in the construction of the narrative is reasonable. To a degree, this seems counterintuitive because the process of narrative writing clearly relies more on intuition than the process of analyzing narrative. Nevertheless, it can be argued that a narrative only counts as a *research* narrative if it is carefully crafted on the basis of a systematic review of data. There is also a reasonable expectation that researchers who use narrative writing as a research method account for their sources of data and for the main steps in the construction of the narrative (see, for example, the extract from Chik and Benson, 2008, above). It is worth noting that reviewers of narrative work are often alert to the possibility of "cherry-picking," or selecting data that supports the researcher's argument, while ignoring data that would problematize or contradict it. It is the researcher's responsibility, therefore, both in narrative writing and the analysis of narratives, to convey a clear sense that data has been analyzed rigorously in their writing.

5.5.2 Trustworthiness

By "trustworthiness" we refer to the rather complex question of the relationship between the findings of narrative inquiry studies and the underlying "realities" they purport to represent. This question can also be posed at two levels. What do stories about language teaching and learning tell us about the reality of language teaching and learning? What happens when researchers write about the stories of others? The first question is partly philosophical and relates to the relationship between representations of reality and the realities they represent. When learners write LLHs, for example, we can reasonably assume that they are writing about things that actually happened, but we can also assume that they are not writing about them exactly *as* they happened. Narratives impose structure and meaning upon the flow of experiences and they cannot, therefore, be interpreted as transparent windows on to the events and processes they represent. Narrative researchers have at times been criticized for this failing (e.g., Denzin, 1989; Pavlenko, 2007) and Nevkapil (2003) has made useful observations in this regard in the context of research on "language biographies."

For Nekvapil (2003) a language biography is "a biographical account in which the narrator makes a language, or languages—and their acquisition and use in particular—the topic of his or her narrative" (p. 64). Drawing on Denzin's (1989: 30) distinction between "life as lived, life as experienced, life as told," he discusses three kinds of findings concerned with:

1. what "things" were like, how events occurred (findings from the sphere of the reality of life),
2. how "things" and events were experienced by the respondents (findings from the sphere of the reality of the subject),
3. how "things" and events are narrated by the respondents (findings from the sphere of the reality of the text). (p. 69)

This implies three levels of focus in narrative inquiry: narrative as text, narrative as the subject's individual or psychological reality, and narrative as an account of the reality of life. The "small story" approach discussed earlier in this chapter, for example, insists that narratives should only be treated as texts. They tell us little, if anything about the people who narrate them (outside the specific interactional context of narration) and even less about the things they tell stories about. We would argue, alongside Nekvapil, however, that narratives do, in fact, tell us a good deal about the reality of experience and life in the context of language teaching and learning. At the same time, researchers need to be aware of these different levels of interpretation and incorporate them into analysis.

Among the featured studies discussed earlier in this chapter, Gao (2010) illustrates how this awareness can be built into an analysis of narratives. Gao treats Zhang Haidi's published narratives as a source of data on the reality of autonomous learning, and reasonably so given the difficulty of investigating long-term processes of language learning by other means. But he also shows that he is aware of the risk of treating her accounts as "factual representations" as "all the texts were socially constructed and some of them were politically motivated" (p. 582). He also adds another layer of analysis by noting differences between the diaries and letters that were published as official propaganda in the early 1980s and the autobiography that was published commercially twenty years later. While the earlier texts highlight the role of "socialist ideals" in Zhang's motivation, the autobiography focuses on Zhang's visions of her "ideal self." Nevertheless, he argues, the carefully edited earlier texts also retain traces of these visions of ideal self and the two sources of motivation come together within the idea that learning languages will make Zhang "useful" to her country.

The second level of trustworthiness refers to the relationship between the researcher and the participants who furnish data for narrative studies. In autobiographical, or first-person, studies this issue does not really arise, because we can trust the researcher to tell the story that he or she wants to tell. This is not the case in biographical, or third-person, studies, where there is always a risk that the original storyteller's intentions and meanings will be distorted in the re-telling for the purposes of research. This is a risk that is best dealt with by explicitly involving research participants at several stages of the research. Barkhuizen (2010) and Chik and Benson (2008), for example, both report that they showed their work to the informant and built their comments into a final stage of data analysis. Liu and Xu (2011: 591) claim that the "trust and rapport" that was built up with the informant during the process of "restorying" enhanced the "trustworthiness" of their research. It is also important for researchers to acknowledge the processes through which narratives pass before they reach the printed page. Menard-Warwick (2004: 299), for example, notes that while the narratives she used were stories of "real-life" experience, they had "twice undergone a shaping process to meet the demands of an audience." First, the participants constructed their accounts according to their interpretations of her "identity as an Anglo teacher" and second she selected parts of the stories that were most relevant to gender and language learning in immigrant communities. She writes, "although the responsibility for selecting and interpreting the narratives is mine, I have tried to represent the tellers in keeping with the ways that they represented themselves to me" (p. 299).

5.5.3 Generalizability

There is often an expectation that research findings should be "generalizable," not simply in the sense that they are applicable to a wide range of contexts, but also in the sense that they make some contribution to theory. Narrative inquiry studies typically limit their claims in these respects, emphasizing their focus on the particular and the individual. This orientation towards the construction of knowledge is also shared with much qualitative research, in which the rich description of particular cases is opposed to the more abstract generalizations of quantitative research. This raises the question, however, of how narrative studies contribute to our knowledge of language teaching and learning—a question that can be answered in a number of ways.

Several of the studies that we have reviewed in this chapter do, in fact, make limited general claims. Gao (2010), for example, claims that his study supports the theoretical assumption that motivation, beliefs, and strategy use are important in autonomous learning. In this instance, evidence for the general theory is found within an individual case study, which also furnishes a richer view of its operation in a specific context. Chik (2011) suggests a limited generalization of a different kind. Her conclusion that language awareness among Hong Kong students develops along a particular path is based on an assumption of "typicality." Because the participants in her study learned English within a cultural and institutional context that is shared by most Hong Kong students, it is reasonable to assume that language awareness develops similarly for other Hong Kong students. This conclusion is essentially a hypothesis that can be tested through further research. The aggregation of narrative data, however, works somewhat differently from the construction of representative samples in quantitative studies. In narrative research, generalization is often a matter of establishing a pattern of shared experience. This is evident, for example, in O'Sullivan's (2010) study, in which she concludes that the textual metaphors she observed, "appear to transcend the cultural and linguistic backgrounds of a range of authors from diverse contexts." In this she sees evidence of "common human experiences of coming to terms with life abroad, which in many of the narratives appear to be experienced in very similar ways" (p. 116). The important point about this statement is that O'Sullivan does not claim that this is the experience of all or many, but only that it is a shared experience that appears to go beyond the particular experiences of any single author.

Barkhuizen (2010) and O'Móchain (2006) differ from these studies in that their conclusions are more limited. Barkhuizen's paper concludes with observations about the research participant and makes no attempt to generalize. O'Móchain concludes in a similar way, but adds a coda to suggest that "a queer narrative approach may prove valuable in providing much-needed affirmation for queer-identifying students, as well as promoting empathetic values and open-ended imaginations of gender and sexuality for all students—especially within institutional or regional contexts in which such issues are rarely discussed openly"

(p. 64). The suggestion, here, is that an approach that appears to have proven effective in one case may well prove effective in others, especially in teaching and learning situations that share some similarities with the one under study. In Barkhuizen's study there is, perhaps, a similar suggestion, albeit an implicit one, that the analysis of Sela's case may have resonances for the analysis of similar cases. As Polkinghorne (1995: 11) argues, "the cumulative effect of narrative reasoning is a collection of individual cases in which thought moves from case to case instead of from case to generalization." In studies where the research outcome is a narrative or a close analysis of a specific narrative, the research "findings" do not come in the form of generalizable propositions, but are constituted by the narrative or analysis as a whole. They may, nevertheless, explicitly or implicitly invite readers to consider points of connection with other narratives and analyses.

6

REPORTING NARRATIVE STUDIES

6.1 Introduction

Although in many cases the "write-up" of a research project begins after the analysis (e.g., in the form of a term paper, a journal article, or a dissertation), it is probably true that planning for the reporting begins right at the start of the research process. In other words, it is built into the design of the study. We see this clearly in studies which follow traditional social science conventions. Table 6.1 illustrates the typical steps involved in both conducting such studies and reporting their findings.

The processes involved in conducting narrative studies are not always so straightforward. As we saw in the previous chapter, the iterative, emergent, and interpretive nature of these studies makes following the conventional sequence of research stages difficult. The same applies to the reporting of the research outcomes. Nonetheless, as Lincoln (1997: 38) says, "even before we have completed a significant period of time in the field, we have already begun contemplating the written work it will produce—a book, several articles, one or more conference presentations." This chapter looks at a range of ways in which narrative inquiry projects are reported. Some of these will be fairly familiar, following as they do the reporting procedures and formats found in qualitative research generally. Others have heeded the call to generate research reports that align more appropriately with a narrative epistemology (i.e., knowing the world and ourselves in it narratively) and a narrative methodology (i.e., approaches to doing narrative inquiry). Smith (2007: 392) says that "narrative researchers have available to them a range of ways in which we might represent our 'findings'," and Polkinghorne (1997: 3) encourages researchers to "experiment" with more appropriate narrative formats in reporting their studies. In this chapter we draw on published narrative inquiry reports to explore some of these formats.

TABLE 6.1 Conventional social science research approach and reporting

Research process	Report organization
1. Developing the topic of the study and the relevant research questions	Introduction
2. Relating research questions to established theories and literature	Literature review
3. Choosing a suitable methodological approach and designing the methods of data collection and analysis	Methodology
4. Collecting and analyzing data	Methodology
5. Determining the findings or results	Findings (and Discussion)
6. Interpreting the findings in relation to established theory and literature	Discussion
7. Drawing conclusions and producing implications	Conclusion

Chapter 5 has already covered quite of bit of ground concerning the presentation of narrative research reports. For example, issues to do with rigor, trustworthiness, and generalizability apply not only to the quality and ethics of data analytical processes, but also to quality and ethics in the presentation of the research outcomes. It is important to bear these in mind when considering the various approaches to reporting discussed below. Section 6.2 provides a general overview of important decisions narrative researchers need to make when planning and preparing their reports. By *report* we mean any form of presentation that reports the process and findings of a narrative inquiry project. These include journal articles, book chapters, term papers, dissertations, conference presentations, dramas, and electronic/multimodal formats. Section 6.3 covers reports which present findings of thematic analyses, and Section 6.4 deals with the reporting of studies that focus on narrative in interaction. Section 6.5 presents an example of an article which is itself in narrative form, and finally, Section 6.6 introduces the idea of crafted narratives.

6.2 From Data to Research Reports

When planning and preparing research reports, decisions have to be made about how best to make claims about the trustworthiness of the research, particularly how to represent the language teaching or learning experiences of the participants—the participants in the study who narrated their lived or imagined stories of experience. This places an enormous responsibility on the researcher—the person who collected, analyzed, and interpreted the data on which the report is to be based. Of course, the researcher has already been involved in decision-making about the generation and analysis of data, sometimes even intimately co-constructing the data with the participants, such as in conversations or narrative interviews. However, research reports expose the quality of the researcher's analysis and interpretations, at least implicitly through what is presented and how. The report, in other words, contains a trace of the researcher's involvement in the entire research process. Clandinin and Connelly describe the difference between data (or what they call field texts) and research reports (research texts) by emphasizing the interpretive work of the researcher:

> Field texts are not, in general, constructed with a reflective intent; rather, they are close to experience, tend to be descriptive, and are shaped around particular events. They have a recording quality to them, whether auditory or visual. Research texts are at a distance from field texts and grow out of the repeated asking of questions concerning meaning and significance. (1998: 170)

Exactly how explicit the researchers' trace should be is one of the questions they need to ask themselves when putting together the report. This is one of a host of questions, all of which have to do with the complex interrelationships among the following six variables (see Figure 6.1): the participant(s), the topic of the research, the researcher(s), the audience, the purpose of the research, and the form of the report. Although each of these is discussed in turn below, it cannot be emphasized enough that it is their interrelationship which shapes the final report.

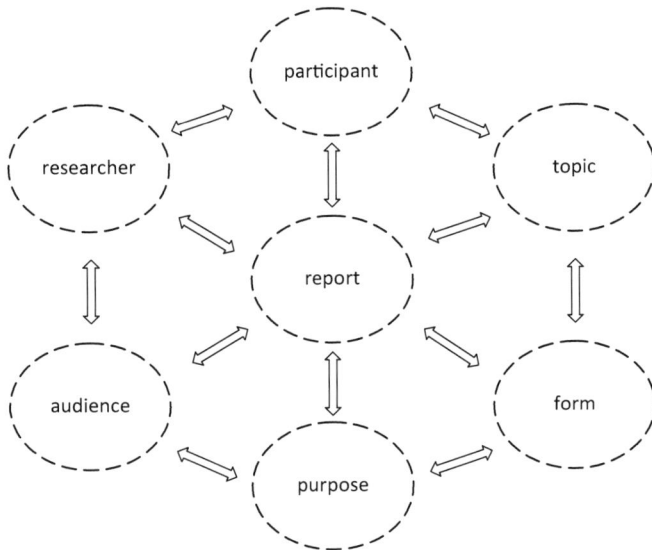

FIGURE 6.1 Significant variables in planning and preparing a research report.

6.2.1 The Participant(s)

The participants are the central characters in any narrative inquiry. The study is about them. It is their lived and imagined experiences that researchers share or "restory" in their reports. In other words, researchers represent those experiences to an audience. Narrative inquiries typically focus on only one or few participants, as in the case of Sakui's (2002, see Chapter 3) self-study of the relationship between her own English teaching and learning experiences. But sometimes there can be multiple participants, as in Chik and Briedbach's (2011b, see Chapter 4) multimodal study of two classes of students in Hong Kong and Germany exchanging reflections about their language learning and professional development. The number will obviously have an influence on how researchers are able to represent participants' experiences in the report text (and we use text here to mean a report which is written, spoken, acted, or visually produced). When deciding how to represent participants' experiences in a narrative inquiry report a researcher typically considers the following questions:

1. What is the nature of my research relationship with the participants? How do I portray and problematize this in the report?
2. How much emphasis do I give to the "voice" of the participants (what they say, either in their own words or as represented by the researcher)?
3. How do I include their words in the report text?
4. How do I balance what the participants narrate in the data with what I want to say about the data?
5. How should I collaborate with the participants when constructing the report?
6. Should I show a draft of the report to the participants?
7. What do I do with the feedback they provide?
8. Have I treated the participants ethically in the report?
9. Have I considered the possible consequences of the report becoming public for the participants and their community?

6.2.2 The Researcher(s)

Tierney (1997) describes a number of narrator options for authors of qualitative research reports. Typically researchers emerge in their reports as "stable" data gatherers who then unproblematically analyze their data and report the findings. In other words, they take on a somewhat mechanical or laboratorial appearance in the text. In some cases they make their presence more visible in the text by using first person 'I' to report on their role in the research process including their interpretation of the data. Or they spend a paragraph or two declaring their subjective stance, usually by providing a brief biographical sketch of "who they are." But even here their narrator position can be noticeably omniscient—that is, they remain personally distant from the actual report and present it from an all-knowing position. Canagarajah (1996: 325) calls instead for "a more sustained and rigorous exploration of the ways the researcher's subjectivity influences the research process."

Polkinghorne points out that the unfolding of the narrative research process is never unproblematic, and furthermore that it is a process in which researchers are inextricably implicated:

> Researchers are the protagonists in the drama of their quests for under-standing. The drama consists of a sequential composition of decisions, actions, chance occurrences, and interactions with subjects and colleagues. Values, desires, inadequacies, skills, and personal characteristics make their appearance at various points in the researcher's performance. (1997: 9)

In addition, researchers themselves are not stable, unchanging technicians. As Lincoln (1997: 40) says, they are "multiple selves": in different contexts, with different participants, for different audiences, and at different times, they construct their researcher selves differently. And when it comes to authoring the research report, Lincoln asks: What "onstage role" do we play in the text? Other questions researchers might ask themselves when preparing the report include:

1. How visible should I be in the research report?
2. What "voice" do I want to project in the report?
3. How do I balance what the participants narrate in the data with what I want to say about the data?
4. How do I want the audience of the report to perceive me?
5. How much detail do I provide about the ups and downs of the research process?
6. Am I being ethical in the way I portray the experiences of the participants?
7. How and to what extent do I portray my relationship with the participants in the text?
8. What will the consequences of my narrator position be for my own development as a researcher?

6.2.3 The Audience

The act of narration implies an audience. In narrative inquiries participants tell their stories to researchers who then restory them for a broader audience. In other words, they represent for the audience the participant's experiences in the reports they construct. Audiences typically range from individuals (e.g., a course instructor or an examiner), to small groups (e.g., conference delegates or school communities), to large often unknown communities (e.g., readers of internation-ally available academic journals). Reporting to these different audiences requires the researcher to imagine his or her audience and to pay special attention to both the *purpose* and *form* of the report so that it engages the audience in the way that the researcher intends. Bell (2011: 582) says that "narrative work resonates well with its audience and appears to be well remembered as a result." This is only true if the researcher has constructed the report with a particular audience and purpose in mind. The following questions regarding the audience might be asked by researchers while preparing their report:

1. Who is my audience for this particular report?
2. How do I construct my report so that I engage my audience with the topic of the study?
3. How do I make the audience connect with the participants' experiences?
4. What will the audience response to my report be?
5. Will the report achieve its intended purpose?
6. How do I make this report readable and memorable?
7. How will the audience perceive me, the researcher?
8. Should I consider constructing multiple reports for different audiences?

6.2.4 The Purpose of the Research

There are many possible reasons why narrative research is disseminated to an audience. Again, knowing or imagining members of the target audience is crucial for ensuring that the report, first, reaches the appropriate audience, and second, engages them to the extent that the purposes of the inquiry are achieved. An obvious purpose of any narrative inquiry report is to benefit the local teaching and learning community in which the inquiry was carried out—to bring about change that leads to professional growth or to the transformation of policies or practices. The particular life experiences of the participants represented in these reports would be immediately meaningful to such audiences, and they would be especially interested in the implications or recommendations stated in the reports. In Xu and Liu's (2009, see Chapter 2) narrative inquiry of a Chinese college EFL teacher's assessment experiences, for example, the authors end their report by suggesting assessment-related changes to teachers' professional development.

On a broader level, reports are written for a discipline's research community. To avoid the 'who cares?' question, these reports also need to make contributions, which may be evident as implications for research methodologies or proposals which advance theory in the field. Barkhuizen's (2010, see Chapter 5) positioning analysis of a Tongan pre-service teacher's small story, for example, proposes extending established methods of this analytical approach—a methodological advancement. In other words, his report had a specific purpose directed at the wider narrative research community. Questions researchers might ask themselves about purpose when preparing their reports include:

1. Am I clear about what the purpose of this report is?
2. How do I convey this purpose to a particular target audience?
3. What is the most appropriate form for this report so that its purpose is clearly articulated?
4. What are my beliefs and feelings concerning the topic of the inquiry?
5. Am I prepared to defend my implications and recommendations?
6. Have I carefully considered what the consequences of any change might be for the community who acted on my report?
7. Is my report making a methodological or theoretical contribution to the research community?
8. Should I produce multiple reports to achieve different purposes?

6.2.5 The Research Topic

Any narrative report is about the meanings participants make of their life experiences. As we have pointed out before in this chapter, the participants are the central characters in the report. But what about these life experiences? What makes them interesting for researchers and consumers of their reports? The answer, of course, is the specific *topic* that the researcher decides to focus on. When starting a narrative inquiry project this topic might be fairly broad—a teaching practice, a language learning history (LLH). As the inquiry progresses, however, the topic normally becomes more refined. The refinement process as well as the specific topic will be evident in the actual report. One might argue that it is the topic, reflected in the title of the report, that attracts the attention of and then makes a connection with the audience. The topic is what they want to know more about. The topic "comes to life" through the represented experiences of the research participants and simultaneously by transfer of those experiences to the lives of the audience. As an illustration, Menezes's (2008, see Chapter 5) multimodal study aimed to explore SLA as a complex system. To do so, she analyzed the LLHs of a group of pre-service English teachers at a university in Brazil. Through these LLHs we learn about the theoretical topic of the inquiry. In Menezes's report, therefore, we are not only told about selected aspects of her participants' language learning stories, but also about how these relate (as articulated by the voice of the researcher/report writer) to SLA as a complex system. Questions researchers might ask about topic when preparing their reports are:

1. Have I clearly articulated my topic in this report?
2. How relevant is this topic in the field of language teaching and learning?
3. What purpose does presenting this topic serve?
4. What audience would be interested in this topic?
5. What form do I use to present this topic to ensure connection with my audience?
6. What do my participants think about my findings in this inquiry?

7. Have I related my topic to other reported work in this field?
8. What contribution does this report make to the field?

6.2.6 The Form of the Report

The remainder of this chapter deals with form in narrative research reporting. The five variables discussed above (see Figure 6.1) are all important in this process, as we have stressed, but it is the textual, oral, or visual product of the report that is delivered to an audience—its physical form. Accessibility and engagement will only be achieved if the report is constructed appropriately for the target audience. But how do we decide which form is most appropriate for a particular audience? And what do we mean by *form* in the first place? The following factors are typically considered when attempting to answer these questions:

1. Polkinghorne (1997: 9) states that "the meaning of research results is not independent of the process that produced them; research findings retain the traces of the productive activities that generated them." To what extent, then, should researchers describe the research journey? How do they balance—in terms of both space and substance—the presentation of the findings with the description of the research process?
2. Polkinghorne (1997) calls reports which have a temporal dimension *diachronic*. Diachronic reports, as well as present findings, detail the development of the research process over time. Data collected early is thus presented early in the report, for example. The report has a "plot"—it tells the story of the research. How much of a research story should researchers tell, then? How do they resolve the tension between following a diachronic approach, associated with narrative inquiry, and the more conventional approach, typical of most qualitative research reports (see the introduction to this chapter)?
3. No matter which of these two approaches is emphasized, the researcher always has to select data to include in the report, and decide how to present it. By necessity, "we are forced to fragment our research" (see Bell, 2011: 580): We have to select from the sometimes vast data set illustrative excerpts that best represent our findings. How much data do we need in order to make trustworthy claims about our interpretations? And how do we format this data? The selection and presentation of data will also have space implications, and most report types have length or time restrictions. Narrative data can take up much space. It can be somewhat of a challenge, therefore, to fit into a limited space both the required illustrative data and sufficient discussion about them.
4. The choice of language style used is another significant factor. As Ely (2007: 571) says, "our language creates reality." What she means is that researchers represent their participants' life experiences by means of the language the researchers use to restory those experiences: the choice of vocabulary, the complexity of sentence structure. What is written or spoken in a report, filtered as it

is through the interpretations and language use of the researcher, is far removed from the narrated stories of the participants (i.e., the data), and even more so from their lived reality (i.e., the actual life events). Researchers' linguistic choices have to be very carefully considered therefore in order to reflect as fairly and thoroughly as possible the life experiences of their participants, and at the same time, to ensure connection with the audience so they too can share in and learn from those experiences.

5. By the *organization* of a research report we mean the sequence and arrangement of the parts that make it up. These parts include: the sections and subsections (with suitable headings); excerpts of narrative data; tables and figures; visual data such as drawings, photographs, and screenshots; and any accompanying material, such as appendices and internet links. Researchers like Ely (2007), Polkinghorne (1997), Nelson (2011a), and Canagarajah (1996) have urged narrative researchers to present their reports in ways more consistent with narrative epistemology and methodology; these include giving the report a temporal dimension, making more explicit the voice of the researcher, experimenting with genres like poetry and drama, and utilizing developments in electronic and multimodal media. One challenge researchers have, however, is overcoming the traditions and conventions of qualitative and narrative research reporting, many of which are upheld by gatekeepers such as dissertation examiners, journal editors, and research funders.

In the next section we take a look at four types of reports. We use illustrative studies to highlight some of the variables discussed above, focusing particularly on the form of reports.

6.3 Reporting Thematic Analysis

Reports that present findings of a thematic analysis are probably the most common in the field of language teaching and learning, and many of them take a very similar form, following closely the conventional social science model illustrated in Table 6.1. This applies not only to research journal articles but also to dissertations and even conference presentations. There *are* variations, but essentially the patterning of both sections and the content within them are fairly consistent. For illustrative purposes we use two narrative studies, the first of which was summarized and discussed in Chapter 2 (Coryell, Clark, and Pomerantz, 2010). The second is a doctoral dissertation (Hacker, 2008). Both collected and analyzed interview data.

Coryell, et al. (2010) were interested in the computer-mediated learning experiences of adult heritage Spanish learners. They investigated why they chose to return to college to learn Spanish, how they experienced their online learning, and how their learning was shaped by their personal connections to both their own heritage and to the Spanish language. The study identifies a "cultural fantasy metanarrative" which tells how the learners desire to learn a "proper Spanish" variety (a standard form as opposed to a more local variety) in order to attain an idealized ("fantasy") Spanish identity. A number of themes (called "fantasy themes" by the authors) contribute to an understanding of this metanarrative. In presenting their report in a research journal, Coryell, et al. organized the article in a fairly conventional way. The sections are as follows:

Title
Abstract
Introduction
Literature review and theoretical framework
    Spanish language maintenance and learning: A sociopolitical perspective
    Languages in contact
    Attitudinal studies
Method
    Participants and data gathering
    Online course context
    Data analysis
The culturally proper ideal metanarrative [i.e., Findings]
    The metanarrative
    Fantasy subtheme: The culturally proper ideal requires the use of true Spanish
    Fantasy subtheme: We have to go backward to go forward
        Fantasy subtheme: The culturally proper ideal requires living linguistically in two worlds, not between them
    The choice to learn online
Discussion and implications
Notes
References
Appendix (Interview protocol)

The Findings section (in italics above) is divided into a number of subsections representing the main *themes* that resulted from the analysis of the data. Schematically, this arrangement is shown in the left-hand column in Table 6.2. A variation of this arrangement is shown in the right-hand column. Here, the Findings section consists of subsections depicting the major *categories* that result from the content analysis, and these are then further divided into the themes that pattern together to make up the categories.

The format in the right-hand column is often found in larger reports, such as MA or PhD dissertations and theses, where the findings are presented in one

TABLE 6.2 Organization of Findings sections

Section: Findings	*Section: Findings*
Subsection: Theme	Subsection: Category #1
Discussion	Theme #1
Excerpt of data	Excerpt of data
Discussion	Discussion
Excerpt of data	etc.
Discussion	Theme #2
etc.	Excerpt of data
	Discussion
Subsection: Theme	etc.
Discussion	
Excerpt of data	Subsection: Category #2
Discussion	Theme #1
Excerpt of data	Excerpt of data
Discussion	Discussion
etc.	etc.
	Theme #2
Same pattern repeated two more times	Excerpt of data
	Discussion
	etc.
	Same pattern repeated

long chapter or a series of separate chapters (one per category). An example is Hacker's (2008) doctoral thesis, which aimed to understand the process of language teacher education learning, i.e., how and what language teacher educators learn in the process of doing their teacher educator work. Her narrative inquiry explored through in-depth narrative interviews the experiences of fifteen teacher educators working in New Zealand tertiary institutions, with varying ages, genders, and levels of teacher education experience. Hacker organized her findings into two chapters. Following a *narrative analysis* approach (see Polkinghorne, 1995, described in Chapter 5), the first of these presented the stories of the teacher educator participants. In these stories of about one to two pages each, Hacker provided biographical information about the teacher educators and also recounted their past and current teacher education experiences. Fifteen separate stories thus made up this chapter. In this chapter, then, readers are introduced to the participants and provided with sufficient personal background information to inform their reading of and enhance their engagement with the content of the next chapter. This chapter first briefly defined the four major categories that made up Hacker's findings, and then each category was discussed and interpreted in detail drawing on both the interview data collected and the relevant theoretical and empirical literature. The chapter was divided into four sections, one for each of the four categories, as follows (Hacker, 2008: vii):

[category #1] Teachers

[theme #1] What and how educators learn

[theme #2] Why this learning dimension for these language teacher educators

[theme #3] The "teachers" learning dimension and narrative constituent in context

[category #2] Teaching

[theme #1] What and how educators learn

[theme #2] Why this learning dimension for these language teacher educators

[theme #3] The "teaching" learning dimension and narrative constituent in context

[category #3] Professional Position

[theme #1] What and how educators learn

[theme #2] Why this learning dimension for these language teacher educators

[theme #3] The "professional position" learning dimension and narrative constituent in context

[category #4] Currency

[theme #1] What and how educators learn

[theme #2] Why this learning dimension for these language teacher educators

[theme #3] The "currency" learning dimension and narrative constituent in context

Within the subsections of the Findings section, in both versions in Table 6.2, excerpts of interview data are presented and discussed in turn. Often these excerpts are included as "blocks" of text, typically formatted as indented paragraphs (in conference Powerpoint presentations they usually take up one slide). They are briefly discussed and then the reporter moves onto the next excerpt. Not all data are included as large, separately indented blocks, however. Sometimes shorter extracts are integrated into the discussion, very much like quoted speech. Following is an example from Hacker, talking about the learning of one of her teacher educator participants:

> A further learning process Hamish engaged in was to attend various courses in tertiary teacher training, offered by his institution's professional development centre. One of them focused on the 'principles and practices of university teaching and learning' (r. 1, 22:17) and was a 'two and a half day seminar on basically different philosophies of learning.' Although some parts were 'a bit navel-gazing,' Hamish commented, 'there were some really good things about it and it caused me to think about "what is my view of education?".' (2008: 164)

Thematic analyses are mainly concerned with the content of narrative data. At the same time any thematic analysis will consider, to varying degrees, the context of the data (both local context as well as macro sociopolitical contexts) and its form. In the latter case, recent attention has been paid to how the data are constructed, what we have called in Chapter 5 (Section 5.3.3) *narrative in interaction*. Discourse analytical approaches have been used to examine these data.

6.4 Reporting on Narrative Interaction

When reporting on how narratives are (co-)constructed in interaction, careful attention is paid to illustrating in detail the performance or practice (De Fina, 2013) of those participating in the storytelling. We saw in Chapter 5 that the analysis focuses explicitly on the language and discourse of the interaction in order to bring to light aspects of language teaching and learning, particularly the identities of those doing the interacting. Reports on such studies thus include both an extensive examination of the narrative text and a discussion of what is learned about the content of that text. Barkhuizen's (2010, see Chapter 5) positioning analysis exemplifies such a reporting approach.

Barkhuizen (2010) selected one small story (an interview extract of 114 lines) for close analysis and included it in the report as an appendix. This was the central text that was examined in the study, and all sections of the report relate directly to it. Following an abstract, an introduction, and a review of relevant narrative research methodology literature, he introduces the key narrator: a pre-service teacher from the Pacific island of Tonga working towards her teaching qualification in New Zealand. The following three sections present the outcome of the three-level positioning analysis (see Figure 6.2). The focus in these sections is explicitly on the discourse of the small story; specifically, how the characters in the story come to life discursively (level 1), how the discourse itself is co-constructed

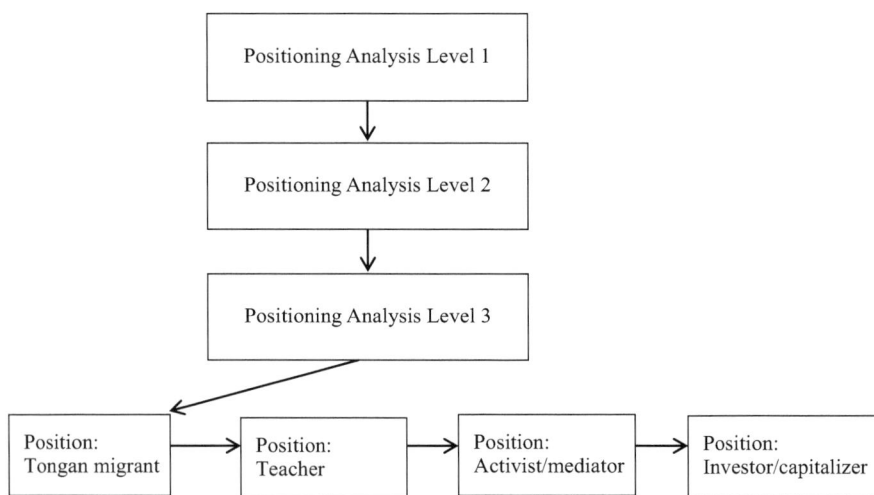

FIGURE 6.2 Organization of Findings sections in Barkhuizen (2010).

by the teacher and the interviewer (level 2), and how what is discovered through this process relates to broader sociopolitical discourses (level 3). Through this process, four narrator *positions* became evident, and these are discussed in turn in the next four sections. Here, Barkhuizen maintains a close connection to the small story text but in addition considers other data collected during the project. There is thus a delicate shift away from exclusive focus on the small story text. Each section in the report builds on the next to develop a coherent account (i.e., the journal article) of the teacher's identities and how they relate to her experiences (real and imagined) of becoming an English teacher.

Simpson (2011) also conducted a positioning analysis of narrative text. This time the small story analyzed was recorded in an adult ESOL classroom in the UK. The interaction takes place between the researcher and a student. During one lesson students were required to search the internet for a folktale from their country of origin and then re-tell it to another person in the class. The researcher, who was observing the class, found himself talking to one of the students about this topic when the student suddenly shifted to tell him rather complicated "tales of her life history" (p. 16). Although the details of these stories are very interesting, what concerns us here is the way the report is structured as a journal article. Like Barkhuizen (2010) the focus text consists of only one excerpt (44 lines), which is in Simpson's case presented within the article itself (i.e., not as an appendix). Simpson then works through levels 1 to 3 of the positioning analysis (as Barkhuizen did; see the top half of Figure 6.2), focusing, as expected, on the discursive construction of the interaction in order to achieve his research aim, which was to examine how aspects of students' life stories outside the classroom are brought into the classroom by negotiating discursive space to do so. In short, the findings are presented in three sections, one for each level of positioning analysis. Unlike Barkhuizen (2010), therefore, the discussion of the narrator positions is done within these three sections (i.e., not extracted to separate sections for more detailed discussion; see bottom half of Figure 6.2). Simpson then ends the article with a short conclusion.

In yet another arrangement, Barkhuizen (2013) reports on a study of an Afrikaans-speaking migrant's language and identity experiences in New Zealand. He conducted three narrative interviews with the adult male participant, Gert, over a period of six years. Barkhuizen was interested in learning about the interconnections between his identity, his language practices (including language maintenance), and social inclusion (the extent to which he felt included economically, socially, and politically in New Zealand society). Again, the findings of the interview analysis are interesting, but our focus here is on the innovative way in which they are presented. Barkhuizen thematically analyzed four short extracts or small stories (about ten lines each) selected from across all the interview data to tell Gert's big story—a broad telling of his migrant life relevant to the research focus (see Figure 6.3). He then analyzed in much more detail, using positioning analysis, one longer small story (100 lines) to investigate further the findings from the more general big story analysis. The thematic

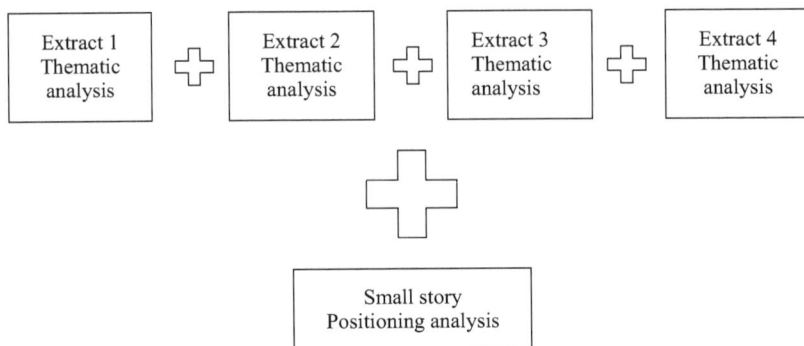

FIGURE 6.3 Organization of selected narrative text in Barkhuizen (2013).

analysis of the content in the four short stories and the positioning analysis of the co-constructed interaction in the longer small story work together to produce a systematic account of Gert's experiences. In a relatively lengthy concluding section, Barkhuizen makes conceptual connections between identity, social inclusion, and language maintenance.

What these three studies show is that reports on discourse analyses of interactional narratives can be organized in a variety of ways, usually dependent on the length and number of data extracts chosen for analysis and included in the report. Always of central importance, however, is the focused attention paid to the text itself. These reports make explicit what text was selected, and why, and show in detail how the text was analyzed to achieve the researcher's aims.

6.5 Reporting in Narrative Form

In our discussion of O'Móchain's (2006) journal article in which he reported on his experiences of exploring gender and sexuality issues in a Japanese college English course (see Chapter 5) we noted that the report was constructed very much like a narrative. The literature review tells the story of the author's reading, for instance, and this is followed by a narrative account of his experiences of actually planning for and teaching the course. We described this process as *narrative writing*. In other words, writing the narrative report is doing the analysis; the plot of the narrative explains whatever it is that the researcher seeks to explain within a particular context of experience. Similarly, as we pointed out in Section 6.2.6 above, there has been a call by narrative researchers to construct their reports diachronically, that is, with a clear temporal dimension (Polkinghorne, 1997). Such reports describe the unfolding of the research process over time, presenting not only the processes involved in the planning, design, and implementation of the project, but also the researcher's involvement (including their practices and reflections) at every step of the way. Here, writing is not so much analysis as it is a report of the analysis.

One report which follows this approach is Casanave (2012). Her article reports on a diary study which recounts her Japanese learning efforts over an eight-year period while living in Japan. She describes her informal learning as "active but low-pressure language learning" (p. 642), and frames the analysis and the report within an ecological perspective. This means that she took into account "the idiosyncratic and fluctuating nature of motivation due to daily contextual, personal, and emotional factors that interacted in unpredictable ways" (p. 642). Her report is an immensely readable document—both interesting and instructive. What follows is a section-by-section breakdown of the article, including a brief commentary within each, where appropriate. There are three points to bear in mind while reading this: (1) The author's voice is clear and present throughout the article. Of course, one would expect this in an autobiographical diary study, but her researcher voice is specially highlighted. (2) The diachronic processes of the research procedures are described in detail and the findings are presented chronologically. While reading the report we are aware, therefore, of how Casanave's learning experiences evolved over time *and* how the inquiry recorded these experiences. (3) The author's observations are frank and personal, filled with emotion and intimacy, but presented with sensitivity and care.

Abstract

Introduction

This section provides a useful and brief background to the aims and context of the study and describes the structure of the article.

Background

Details of Casanave's language learning history are presented in this section, and she also introduces the term *dabbling*: a "nonintensive engagement" (p. 644) with language learning.

What Kind of Study is This?

Casanave describes her study as a diary study (see Chapter 3), but with some differences to those published previously: Her study is longitudinal, covering a period of eight years; it accounts for learning outside the classroom; it is a tale of an "ordinary person"—a language teacher living in a foreign country; and it takes an ecological approach to analysis and presentation.

Commentary on Research from an Ecological Perspective

Here Casanave briefly reviews literature on motivation, the ecology of language development, and the power of narrative research. She makes the very important point that *context* is "the focal milieu, including the physical and emotional . . . within which all experience happens and is given meaning" (p. 646). Her report promises and turns out to be rich in contextual detail.

The Japan Journals

This section describes how and when the journals were written, and how they were analyzed. Procedures of the thematic analysis are explained and integrated with personal reflections on these.

Setting

Rich contextual details (e.g., physical location, relationships, sociopolitical concerns) are given of the university where Casanave worked and of the neighborhood where she lived. She includes her reflections on her emotions in relation to these contexts.

Overview of My Goals for Self-Study in Japan

Casanave tells of her personal goals for learning Japanese and how these were to be accomplished: no formal classes, schedules, or assessment; building a vocabulary that was important to her in her immediate environment; and being able to take care of her survival needs as a foreigner living and working in Japan.

Ecologically Influenced Dabbling

In conventional social science journal articles we would probably consider this section the start of the report on the findings of the study. However, as readers we have already been immersed in the narrative of the study since the beginning of the article. The outcome of the thematic analysis cannot be separated from the processes of the research, the researcher's reflections on these, and the rich description of the academic, physical, personal, and emotional context of the subject matter. We are told by the researcher in this section that four interrelated themes are to be presented in the subsections that follow.

Analytical curiosity

This is the first of the four themes sections. As with the others, excerpts from the journals are presented *chronologically* (by date of appearance in the journals over the years) and examined for meaning. Throughout these four sections reference is made to appendices, which present actual examples of handwritten journal entries.

Influences out of my control
Informants and tutors
Having fun

Reflections on an Ecology of Effort

This is the "official" concluding section of the article. Casanave makes connections here with other diary studies set in Japan and reflects on how the ecological perspective she employed relates to her own study.

Epilogue

In this final section, Casanave adds a few short personal reflections written sometime after drafting the article and returning to the US. She reports on her journal writing, which she continues to do, on the people she misses in Japan, and her Japanese language use when visiting Japan.

ACKNOWLEDGEMENTS
THE AUTHOR
REFERENCES
APPENDICES

This report is diachronic in the sense that it includes a number of interconnecting temporal threads: specifically, the story of the research process (how the study was carried out), the stories of Japanese learning and use told in the diary data (the excerpts included in the article), and Casanave's representation of her story (what she says about her story and about how she tells it in the article). In addition, the study is soundly framed theoretically within an ecological perspective. This article, therefore, is a good example of the kind of narrative report which represents "the research process in all its concreteness and complexity" (Canagarajah, 1996: 327) and in which "the subjectivity of the researchers—with their complex values, ideologies, and experiences—shapes the research activity and findings" (p. 324).

6.6 Reporting Crafted Narratives

Ely (2007: 571) says simply about narrative research reporting, "There are numerous ways for us to report." In addition to the approaches presented so far in this chapter, which range from fairly conventional social science formats to heavily contextualized, diachronic diary studies, Ely suggests alternative rhetorical forms more appropriate for presenting the findings of narrative inquiry, such as poetry, stories, and drama. These forms constitute the actual written or performed reports that are presented to an audience. Ely says that they "allow for a communication of different meaning and emphases" (p. 572), and Nelson (2011a) argues that such "crafted" representations "may enrich the field [of language teaching and learning] by engaging those who—for myriad reasons—find it challenging to participate in research conversations as these are currently structured." These alternative, or innovative, forms, then: (a) have the potential to be engaging and accessible to a wider audience, (b) share the meanings of participants' experiences, including their emotions and ideas, in ways consistent with a narrative epistemology and methodology and which more conventional modes of reporting struggle to do, and (c) make available opportunities for collaborative construction and performance (Nelson, 2011a). However, reporting in innovative ways no doubt presents some challenges. For instance, not all audiences will appreciate deviations from anticipated, traditional forms, such as examiners of research dissertations or reviewers of manuscripts submitted to research journals. Some may perceive crafted narratives as trivial or lighthearted, and thus not serious scientific work. One solution to this dilemma is to consider constructing multiple reports, with various forms constructed to suit particular audiences.

Which is what Nelson (2011a) did. Starting with a large data set including classroom observations and interviews with teachers and learners, Nelson crafted a playscript which she called *Queer as a Second Language* (this process is more fully described in Nelson, 2013). Her aim was to perform the play to an audience of teachers at an international conference (Nelson, 2011b). She assumed many of them would not have engaged with her other research reports, such as her books and journal articles. In crafting the playscript, Nelson used her data to develop five main composite characters from the 110 actual research participants. The following excerpt (Nelson, 2011a: 475–6) is based on an actual classroom discussion. Note, the script is not an exact reproduction of the discussion, but was "edited for conciseness, clarity, and dramatic momentum" (p. 479).

[This is an excerpt from Scene 3. Mr. V is a 62-year-old man from Vietnam, Mi-Young and Pablo are his classmates, and Tony is their teacher.]
BELL SOUNDS. STUDENTS turn towards TONY.

MR. V: One day a friend ask me to go to bar after work. After a few minutes, he told me "Do you see there's no woman in this bar?" I was surprised. Then one man . . . come to me. And fluh with me. *(MI-YOUNG and PABLO laugh)*

TONY: What?

MR. V: Come to me and fluh.

TONY: And WHAT?

PABLO: *(spelling the word in a friendly way to help TONY understand)* F–L–I–R–T.

TONY:	*(delighted)* Flirted with you! *(ALL laugh)* Our vocabulary word!
MR. V:	My friend whisper something on the man's ear, then the man, he walk off.
TONY:	Uh-huh.
MR. V:	I ask my friend "What you say?" My friend said "I told him we got married a few days ago, so we are on honeymoon." *(ALL laugh)*

As this excerpt illustrates, playscripts dramatize the storytelling that takes place between people in the course of social interaction: in this case, a classroom discussion. The result is an engaging representation of the meaning making that took place during the original interaction.

A second example of crafted narratives comes in the form of poetry. In Nelson's (2011a) article she presents a poem which she wrote based on a classroom discussion that took place in a class she was teaching. The discussion so interested her that after the class she wrote down from memory the students' comments, and later composed these into a story (essentially a list of their comments). Years later when she came across this list she reshaped it into a poem. Poems, says Ely (2007: 575), "streamline, encapsulate, and define, usually with brevity but always with the intent to plumb the heart of the matter . . . [they] spotlight particular events in ways that lift them out of the often overwhelming flood of life so that they can be understood as part of that." Nelson's poem, a teacher's poem, captures a moment of classroom life of a particular group of people and represents it to an audience in a compact, engaging form.

The poem below was written by an English teacher in Chile who was studying towards a graduate teacher education qualification. It was included in a written course assignment which required teachers to analyze a set of personal reflections (written journal entries, poems, drawings, Powerpoint slides) included in a narrative portfolio they had developed during the four-week course. The assignment took the form of a narrative report in which the teachers interpreted their teacher identities as represented in their portfolios, focusing particularly on significant past events, relationships with people, classroom experiences, and imagined futures. The following poem was included in a report which had as its main theme the volatile educational climate in Chile.

I imagine a utopian education

I'm waiting for an inclusive education, yes
I'm waiting for a quality education, yes
I'm waiting for a tolerant education, yes
I'm waiting for an equal education, yes
Not only me but many others wait with me . . .

I look so much inequality
I look so much difference and indifference
I look so much fighting
I look so much indolence
Not only me but many others look with me . . .

I feel courage for the students of my country
I feel the union of the students of my country
I respect my country students
I feel proud of my country students
Not only me but many others feel with me . . .

In the poem the teacher places herself firmly within the political upheavals of the educational system, commenting on its inequality and other shortcomings. She also expresses her loyalty and respect, and imagines a future where many of the unsettling issues have been resolved. In the poem, she is not alone—others share her feelings, her observations, and her imaginings of a better future. The teacher's own voice comes through strongly in this powerful poem, which was included in the course assignment with extracts of other portfolio "data," all of which were integrated with interpretive commentary. Narrative reports of this kind invite opportunities for the construction and inclusion of crafted narratives. There is flexibility and tolerance. In other reporting contexts, however, as we have pointed out, this might not always be the case.

6.7 Conclusion

This chapter has discussed some of the important variables, among many others, which are commonly considered when constructing narrative research reports: the participant(s), the topic of the research, the researcher(s), the audience, the purpose of the research, and the form of the report. What has become clear is that there is no single or agreed upon way of reporting the various kinds of narrative inquiry. As we have mentioned earlier, this applies also more generally to doing narrative inquiry. For some, this fluidity of approach or lack of definitive methodological guidelines may be the cause of some concern or even anxiety: How *do* we do narrative inquiry? What *are* its methods? Why narrative inquiry and not other methods? For others, the situation is more comforting because, first, they do not feel the pressure to master a body of knowledge they may be unfamiliar with or need to understand in order to make progress, and second, it allows them an opportunity to explore new methodological territory and to locate themselves within it. This book has opened up this narrative inquiry landscape in the field of language teaching and learning by providing a broad overview or a map of the terrain within which we hope readers will begin to locate their (proposed) work.

One way we did this was to present throughout the book numerous featured studies to illustrate ways in which data for narrative inquiry projects have been collected and analyzed, and to show how the findings from these studies have been reported. Our main reason for using this strategy was to show readers research that has already been screened by a critical eye, be it an article reviewer or a dissertation examiner. These illustrative narrative studies, therefore, serve as exemplars for those planning their own research projects.

Integrated with the exemplars is our commentary on them. Here we have been selective so that what we have said not only summarizes the research and highlights the points we were trying to make about it, but we also hoped that it would be instructive, that is, we shaped the commentary so that it suggested to readers ways for approaching their data collection and analysis and research reporting (this, besides the more implicit instructive function of the summaries themselves). In other words, our aim in this book was to provide an overview of narrative inquiry in language teaching and learning *and* to suggest to readers ways of actually doing their own narrative inquiry. This approach to research is fairly new in our field, but it is an exciting and fast developing one. We hope that this book has generated in readers an inquisitiveness and desire to explore it further.

REFERENCES

Aoki, N. (2002). Teachers' Conversation with Partial Autobiographies. *Hong Kong Journal of Applied Linguistics*, 7 (2), 152–68.

Aoki, N., with Hamakawa, Y. (2003). Asserting Our Culture: Teacher Autonomy from a Feminist Perspective. In D. Palfreyman & R.C. Smith (Eds.), *Learner Autonomy Across Cultures: Language Education Perspectives* (pp. 240–53). Basingstoke, UK: Palgrave Macmillan.

Armour, W.S. (2001). 'This Guy is Japanese Stuck in a White Man's Body': A Discussion of Meaning-Making, Identity Slippage, and Cross-Cultural Adaptation. *Journal of Multilingual and Multicultural Development*, 22 (1), 1–18.

Armour, W.S. (2004) Becoming a Japanese Language Learner, User, and Teacher: Revelations from Life History Research. *Journal of Language, Identity, and Education*, 3 (2), 101–25.

Atkinson, R. (1998). *The Life Story Interview*. Thousand Oaks, CA: Sage Publications.

Bailey, K.M. (1983). Competitiveness and Anxiety in Adult Second Language Learning: Looking at and Through the Diary Studies. In H.W. Seliger & M.H. Long (Eds.), *Classroom Oriented Research in Second Language Acquisition* (pp. 67–102). Rowley, MA: Newbury House.

Bailey, K.M. (1990). The Use of Diary Studies in Teacher Education Programmes. In J.C. Richards & D. Nunan (Eds.), *Second Language Teacher Education* (pp. 215–26), Cambridge: Cambridge University Press.

Baker, S.C., & MacIntyre, P. (2000). The Role of Gender and Immersion in Communication and Second Language Orientations. *Language Learning*, 50 (2), 311–41.

Bamberg, M. (1997). Positioning Between Structure and Performance. *Journal of Narrative and Life History*, 7 (1–4), 335–42.

Bamberg, M. (2006). Stories: Big or Small: Why Do We Care? *Narrative Inquiry*, 16 (1), 139–47.

Bamberg, M. (2007). Stories: Big or Small: Why Do We Care? In M. Bamberg (Ed.), *Narrative—State of the Art* (pp. 165–74). Amsterdam: John Benjamins.

Bamberg, M., & Georgakopoulou, A. (2008). Small Stories as a New Perspective in Narrative and Identity Analysis. *Text and Talk*, 28 (3), 377–96.

Barcelos, A.M.F. (2008). Learning English: Students' Beliefs and Experiences in Brazil. In P. Kalaja, V. Menezes, & A.M.F. Barcelos (Eds.), *Narratives of Learning and Teaching EFL* (pp. 35–48). Basingstoke, UK: Palgrave Macmillan.

Barkhuizen, G. (2006). Immigrant Parents' Perceptions of their Children's Language Practices: Afrikaans Speakers Living in New Zealand. *Language Awareness, 15* (2), 63–79.

Barkhuizen, G. (2008a). A Narrative Approach to Exploring Context in Language Teaching. *English Language Teaching Journal, 62* (3), 231–39.

Barkhuizen, G. (2008b). Imagined Success of Adult Migrant and Refugee English Learners. Paper presented at the Applied Linguistics Association of New Zealand (ALANZ) Annual Symposium, Auckland, New Zealand.

Barkhuizen, G. (2009). Topics, Aims, and Constraints in English Teacher Research: A Chinese Case Study. *TESOL Quarterly, 43* (1), 113–25.

Barkhuizen, G. (2010). An Extended Positioning Analysis of a Pre-service Teacher's *Better Life* Small Story. *Applied Linguistics, 31* (2), 282–300.

Barkhuizen, G. (Ed.). (2011). Narrative Research in TESOL. Special Issue of *TESOL Quarterly, 45* (3).

Barkhuizen, G. (2013). Maintenance, Identity and Social Inclusion Narratives of an Afrikaans Speaker Living in New Zealand. *International Journal of the Sociology of Language, 222*, 77–100.

Barkhuizen, G., & de Klerk, V. (2006). Imagined Identities: Pre-immigrants' Narratives on Language and Identity. *International Journal of Bilingualism, 10* (3), 277–99.

Barkhuizen, G., & Hacker, P. (2008). Inquiring into Learning about Narrative Inquiry in Language Teacher Education. *New Zealand Studies in Applied Linguistics, 14* (1), 36–52.

Barkhuizen, G., & Wette, R. (2008). Narrative Frames for Investigating the Experiences of Language Teachers. *System, 36* (3), 372–87.

Barnard, R., & Nguyen, G.V. (2010). Task-Based Language Teaching (TBLT): A Vietnamese Case Study Using Narrative Frames to Elicit Teachers' Beliefs. *Language Education in Asia, 1* (1), 77–86.

Barry, L. (2002). *One Hundred Demons*. Seattle: Sasquatch Books.

Bathmaker, A-M., & Harnett, P. (Eds.). (2010). *Exploring Learning, Identity and Power Through Life History and Narrative Research*. London: Routledge.

Beatty, K. (2010). *Teaching and Researching Computer-Assisted Language Learning*. Second edition. Harlow, UK: Longman.

Belcher, D., & Connor, U. (Eds.). (2001). *Reflections on Multiliterate Lives*. Clevedon, UK: Multilingual Matters.

Bell, J.S. (1997). *Literacy, Culture and Identity*. New York: Peter Lang.

Bell, J.S. (2002). Narrative Inquiry: More than Just Telling Stories. *TESOL Quarterly, 36* (2), 207–18.

Bell, J.S. (2011). Reporting and Publishing Narrative Inquiry in TESOL: Challenges and Rewards. *TESOL Quarterly, 45* (3), 575–84.

Bellingham, L. (2004). Is There Language Acquisition after 40? Older Learners Speak Up. In P. Benson & D. Nunan (Eds.), *Learners' Stories: Difference and Diversity in Language Learning* (pp. 56–68). Cambridge: Cambridge University Press.

Benson, P. (2004). (Auto)biography and Learner Diversity. In P. Benson & D. Nunan (Eds.), *Learners' Stories: Difference and Diversity in Language Learning* (pp. 2–21). Cambridge: Cambridge University Press.

Benson, P. (2011). Language Learning Careers as a Unit of Analysis in Narrative Research. *TESOL Quarterly, 45* (3), 545–53.

Benson, P., & Cooker, L. (2013). The Social and the Individual in Applied Linguistics Research. In P. Benson & L. Cooker (Eds.), *The Applied Linguistic Individual: Sociocultural Approaches to Autonomy, Agency and Identity* (pp. 1–16). London: Equinox.

Benson, P., & Gao, X. (2008). One Country, Two Learners: Biographical Research in a Chinese Context. *Asian Journal of English Language Teaching, 18,* 41–66.

Benson, P., & Nunan, D. (Eds.). (2002). The Experience of Language Learning. Special Issue of the *Hong Kong Journal of Applied Linguistics,* 7 (2).

Benson, P., & Nunan, D. (Eds.). (2004). *Learners' Stories: Difference and Diversity in Language Learning.* Cambridge: Cambridge University Press.

Benson, P., Barkhuizen, G., Bodycott, P., & Brown, J. (2012). Study Abroad and the Development of Second Language Identities. *Applied Linguistics Review, 3* (1), 173–93.

Benson, P., Barkhuizen, G., Bodycott, P., & Brown, J. (2013). *Second Language Identity in Narratives of Study Abroad.* Basingstoke, UK: Palgrave Macmillan.

Benson, P., Chik, A., Gao, X., Huang, J., & Wang, W. (2009). Qualitative Research in 10 Language Teaching and Learning Journals, 1997–2006. *Modern Language Journal, 93* (1), 79–90.

Benson, P., Chik, A., & Lim, H-Y. (2003). Becoming Autonomous in an Asian Context: Autonomy as a Sociocultural Process. In D. Palfreyman & R.C. Smith (Eds.), *Learner Autonomy Across Cultures* (pp. 23–40). London: Palgrave Macmillan.

Bertaux, D. (Ed.). (1981). *Biography and Society: The Life History Approach in the Social Sciences.* Beverly Hills, CA: Sage.

Block, D. (1996). A Window on the Classroom: Classroom Events Viewed from Different Angles. In K.M. Bailey & D. Nunan (Eds.), *Voices from the Language Classroom* (pp. 168–94). Cambridge: Cambridge University Press.

Block, D. (1998). Tale of a Language Learner. *Language Teaching Research, 2* (2), 148–76.

Block, D. (2000). Problematizing Interview Data: Voices in the Mind's Machine? *TESOL Quarterly, 34* (4), 757–63.

Block, D. (2002). Destabilized Identities and Cosmopolitanism across Language and Cultural Borders: Two Case Studies. *Hong Kong Journal of Applied Linguistics,* 7 (2), 1–19.

Block, D. (2003). *The Social Turn in Second Language Acquisition.* Edinburgh: Edinburgh University Press.

Bogdan, R.C., & Biklen, S.K. (2006). *Qualitative Research for Education. An Introduction to Theory and Methods.* Fifth edition. London: Pearson.

Bormann, E.G. (1985). Symbolic Convergence Theory: A Communication Formulation. *Journal of Communication, 35* (4), 128–38.

Brockmeier, J., & Carbaugh, D. (Eds.). (2001). *Narrative and Identity: Studies in Autobiography, Self and Culture.* Amsterdam: John Benjamins.

Brooks, P. (1979). Fictions of the Wolfman: Freud and Narrative Understanding. *Diacritics, 9* (1), 71–81.

Bruner, J. (1986). *Actual Minds: Possible Worlds.* Cambridge, MA: Harvard University Press.

Bruner, J. (1990). *Acts of Meaning.* Cambridge, MA: Harvard University Press.

Cadman, K., & Brown, J. (2011). TESOL and TESD in Remote Aboriginal Australia: The 'True' Story? *TESOL Quarterly, 45* (3), 440–62.

Cameron, D. (2000). Difficult Subjects. *Critical Quarterly, 42* (4), 89–94.

Campbell, C. (1996). Socializing with the Teachers and Prior Language Learning Experience: A Diary Study. In K.M. Bailey & D. Nunan (Eds.), *Voices from the Language Classroom* (pp. 201–23). Cambridge: Cambridge University Press.

Canagarajah, S. (1996). From Critical Research Practice to Critical Research Reporting. *TESOL Quarterly, 30* (2), 321–31.

Carter, B.A. (2002). Helping Learners Come of Age: Learner Autonomy in a Caribbean Context. *Hong Kong Journal of Applied Linguistics, 7* (2), 20–38.

Casanave, C.P. (2012). Diary of a Dabbler: Ecological Influences on an EFL Teacher's Efforts to Study Japanese Informally. *TESOL Quarterly, 46* (4), 642–70.

Casanave, C.P., & Schecter, S.R. (Eds.). (1997). *On Becoming a Language Educator: Personal Essays on Professional Development.* Mahwah, NJ: Lawrence Erlbaum.

Case, R.E. (2004). Forging Ahead into New Social Networks and Looking Back to Past Social Identities: A Case Study of a Foreign-Born English as a Second Language Teacher in the United States. *Urban Education, 39* (2), 125–48.

Casey, K. (1995). The New Narrative Research in Education. *Review of Research in Education, 21,* 211–53.

Chamberlayne, P., Bornat, J., & Wengraf, T. (Eds.). (2000). *The Turn to Biographical Methods in Social Science: Comparative Issues and Examples.* London: Routledge.

Chase, S.E. (2003). Taking Narrative Seriously: Consequences for Method and Theory in Interview Studies. In Y.S. Lincoln & N.K. Denzin (Eds.), *Turning Points in Qualitative Research: Tying Knots in a Handkerchief* (pp. 273–96). Walnut Creek, CA: Altamira Press.

Chen, J. (2002). Commander and Serviceman—The Story of Kim. *Hong Kong Journal of Applied Linguistics, 7* (2), 73–90.

Chik, A. (2007). From Learner Identity to Learner Autonomy: A Biographical Study of Two Hong Kong Learners of English. In P. Benson (Ed.), *Learner Autonomy 8: Insider Perspectives on Autonomy in Language Teaching and Learning* (pp. 41–60). Dublin: Authentik.

Chik, A. (2008). Native English-speaking Students in Hong Kong EFL Classrooms: A Case Study. *Innovation in Language Learning and Teaching, 2* (1), 18–32.

Chik, A. (2011). Learner Language Awareness Development among Asian Learners and Implications for Teacher Education. In S. Breidbach, D. Elsner, & A. Young (Eds.), *Language Awareness in Teacher Education: Cultural-political and Socio-educational Dimension.* Berlin: Peter Lang.

Chik, A. (forthcoming). Constructing a German Learner Identity On and Offline. In D. bendroth-Timmer & E-M. Hennig (Eds.), *Plurilingualism and Multiliteracies: International Research on Identity Construction in Language Education.* Berlin: Peter Lang.

Chik, A. (forthcoming). Popular Culture and Digital Worlds. In J. Rowsell & K. Pahl (Eds.), *The Routledge Handbook of Literacy Studies.* New York: Routledge.

Chik, A., & Benson, P. (2008). Frequent Flyer: A Narrative of Overseas Study in English. In P. Kalaja, V. Menezes, & A.M.F. Barcelos (Eds.), *Narratives of Learning and Teaching EFL* (pp. 155–68). Basingstoke, UK: Palgrave Macmillan.

Chik, A., & Breidbach, S. (2011a). Identity, Motivation and Autonomy: A Tale of Two Cities. In G. Murray, X. Gao, & T. Lamb (Eds.), *Identity, Motivation and Autonomy in Language Learning* (pp. 145–59). Bristol, UK: Multilingual Matters.

Chik, A., & Breidbach, S. (2011b). Online Language Learning Histories Exchange: Hong Kong and German Perspectives. *TESOL Quarterly, 45* (3), 553–64.

Clandinin, D.J., & Connelly, F.M. (1994). Personal Experience Methods. In N.K. Denzin & Y.S. Lincoln (Eds.), *Handbook of Qualitative Research* (pp. 413–27). Thousand Oaks, CA: Sage.

Clandinin, D.J., & Connelly, F.M. (1998). Personal Experience Methods. In N.K. Denzin & Y.S. Lincoln (Eds.), *Collecting and Interpreting Qualitative Materials* (pp. 150–78). Thousand Oaks, CA: Sage.

Clandinin, D.J., & Connelly, F.M. (2000). *Narrative Inquiry: Experience and Story in Qualitative Research.* San Francisco: Jossey-Bass.

Coffey, S. (2010). Stories of Frenchness: Becoming a Francophile. *Language and Intercultural Communication, 10* (2), 119–36.

Coffey, S., & Street, B. (2008). Narrative and Identity in the Language Learning Project. *The Modern Language Journal, 92* (3), 452–64.

Connelly, F.M., & Clandinin, J. (1990). Stories of Experience and Narrative Inquiry. *Educational Researcher, 19* (5), 2–14.

Connor, U. (1999). Learning to Write Academic Prose in a Second Language: A Literacy Autobiography. In G. Braine (Ed.), *Non-native Educators in English Language Teaching* (pp. 29–42). Mahwah, NJ: Lawrence Erlbaum.

Corbin, J., & Strauss, A. (2008). *Basics of Qualitative Research: Techniques and Procedures for Developing Grounded Theory.* Third edition. Los Angeles, CA: Sage.

Coryell, J.E., Clark, M.C., & Pomerantz, A. (2010). Cultural Fantasy Narratives and Heritage Language Learning: A Case Study of Adult Heritage Learners of Spanish. *The Modern Language Journal, 94* (3), 453–69.

Cotterall, S. (2004). 'It's Just Rules . . . That's All it is at This Stage. . . .' In P. Benson & D. Nunan (Eds.), *Learners' Stories: Difference and Diversity in Language Learning* (pp. 101–18). Cambridge: Cambridge University Press.

Cotterall, S. (2008). Passion and Persistence: Learning English in Akita. In P. Kalaja, V. Menezes, & A.M.F. Barcelos (Eds.), *Narratives of Learning and Teaching EFL* (pp. 113–27). Basingstoke, UK: Palgrave Macmillan.

Curtis, A., & Romney, M. (Eds.). (2006). *Color, Race, and English Language Teaching: Shades of Meaning.* Mahwah, NJ: Lawrence Erlbaum.

DaSilva Iddings, A.C., Haught, J., & Devlin, R. (2005). Multimodal Rerepresentations of Self and Meaning for Second Language Learners in English-dominant Classrooms. In J.K. Hall, G. Vitanova, & L. Marchenkova (Eds.), *Dialogue with Bakhtin on Second and Foreign Language Learning: New Perspectives* (pp. 33–53). Mahwah, NJ: Lawrence Erlbaum.

Davies, B., & Harré, R. (1990). Positioning: The Discursive Production of Selves. *Journal for the Theory of Social Behaviour, 20* (1), 43–63.

De Fina, A. (2013). Narratives as Practices: Negotiating Identities through Storytelling. In G. Barkhuizen (Ed.), *Narrative Research in Applied Linguistics.* Cambridge: Cambridge University Press.

De Fina, A. & Georgakopoulou, A. (2012). *Analyzing Narrative: Discourse and Sociolinguistic Perspectives.* Cambridge: Cambridge University Press.

Denzin, N.K. (1989). *Interpretive Biography.* Newbury Park, CA: Sage.

Dörnyei, Z. (2007). *Research Methods in Applied Linguistics: Quantitative, Qualitative, and Mixed Methodologies.* Oxford: Oxford University Press.

Dufva, H., Aro, M., Alanen, R., & Kalaja, P. (2011). Voices of Literacy, Images of Books— Sociocognitive Approach to Multimodality in Learner Beliefs. *ForumSprache, 6,* 58–74.

Ellis, C., & Bochner, A.P. (2000). Autoethnography, Personal Narrative, Reflexivity. In N.K. Denzin & Y.S. Lincoln. (Eds.), *Handbook of Qualitative Research* (pp. 733–68). Second edition. Thousand Oaks, CA: Sage.

Ellis, E.M. (2004). The Invisible Multilingual Teacher: The Contribution of Language Background to Australian ESL Teachers' Professional Knowledge and Beliefs. *The International Journal of Multilingualism, 1* (2), 90–108.

Ely, M. (2007). In-forming Re-presentations. In D.J. Clandinin (Ed.), *Handbook of Narrative Inquiry: Mapping a Methodology* (pp. 567–98). Thousand Oaks, CA: Sage.

Faerch, C., & Kasper, G. (1987). *Introspection in Second Language Research.* Clevedon, UK: Multilingual Matters.

Firth, A., & Wagner, J. (1997). On Discourse, Communication, and Some Fundamental Concepts in SLA Research. *Modern Language Journal, 81* (3), 285–300.

Fivush, R., & Haden, C.A. (2003). Introduction: Autobiographical Memory, Narrative, and Self. In R. Fivush & C.A. Haden (Eds.), *Autobiographical Memory and the Construction of a Narrative Self: Development and Cultural Perspectives* (pp. vii-xiv). Mahwah, NJ: Lawrence Erlbaum.

Fries, S. (1998). Different Phases: A Personal Case Study in Language Adjustment and Children's Bilingualism. *International Journal of the Sociology of Language, 13* (3), 129–41.

Gao, X. (2010). Autonomous Language Learning Against All Odds. *System, 38* (4), 580–90.

Gao, Y., Li, Y., & Li, W. (2002). EFL Learning and Self-identity Construction: Three Cases of Chinese College English Majors. *Asian Journal of English Language Teaching, 12,* 95–119.

Giddens, A. (1991). *Modernity and Self-identity: Self and Society in the Late Modern Age.* Stanford, CA: Stanford University Press.

Glaser, B.G., & Strauss, A.L. (1967). *The Discovery of Grounded Theory: Strategies for Qualitative Research.* Chicago: Aldine.

Golombek, P.R., & Johnson, K.E. (2004). Narrative Inquiry as a Mediational Space: Examining Emotional and Cognitive Dissonance in Second-language Teachers' Development. *Teachers and Teaching: Theory and Practice, 10* (3), 307–27.

Goodson, I., & Sikes, P. (2001). *Life History Research in Educational Settings: Learning from Lives.* Buckingham, UK: Open University Press.

Hacker, P. (2008). *Understanding the Nature of Language Teacher Educator Learning: Substance, Narrative Essence and Contextual Reality.* Unpublished doctoral dissertation, University of Auckland, Auckland, New Zealand.

Hayes, D. (2010). Duty and Service: Life and Career of a Tamil Teacher of English in Sri Lanka. *TESOL Quarterly, 44* (1), 58–83.

He, A.E. (2002). Learning English in Different Linguistic and Socio-cultural Contexts. *Hong Kong Journal of Applied Linguistics, 7* (2), 107–21.

Heigham, J., & Croker, R. (Eds.) (2009). *Qualitative Research in Applied Linguistics.* Basingstoke, UK: Palgrave Macmillan

Hinton, L. (2001). Involuntary Language Loss among Immigrants: Asian-American Linguistic Autobiographies. In J.E. Alatis & A.H. Tan (Eds.), *Georgetown University Roundtable on Languages and Linguistics 1999* (pp. 203–52). Washington, DC: Georgetown University Press.

Hoffman, E. (1989). *Lost in Translation: A Life in a New Language.* London: Penguin.

Holmes, J., & Marra, M. (2011). Harnessing Storytelling as a Sociopragmatic Skill: Applying Narrative Research to Workplace English Courses. *TESOL Quarterly, 45* (3), 510–34.

Johnson, K.E. & Golombek, P.R. (Eds.). (2002). *Teachers' Narrative Inquiry as Professional Development.* Cambridge: Cambridge University Press.

Johnston, B. (1999). The Expatriate Teacher as Postmodern Paladin. *Research in the Teaching of English, 34* (2), 255–80.

Josselson, R. (1993). A Narrative Introduction. In R. Josselson & A. Lieblich (Eds.), *The Narrative Study of Lives* (pp. ix-xv). Thousand Oaks, CA: Sage.

Kalaja, P., Alanen, R., & Dufva, H. (2008). Self-Portraits of EFL Learners: Finnish Students Draw and Tell. In P. Kalaja, V. Menezes, & A.M.F. Barcelos (Eds.), *Narratives of Learning and Teaching EFL* (pp. 186–98). Basingstoke, UK: Palgrave Macmillan.

Kalaja, P., Menezes, V., & Barcelos, A.M.F. (Eds.). (2008). *Narratives of Learning and Teaching EFL*. Basingstoke, UK: Palgrave Macmillan.

Kanno, Y. (2000). Bilingualism and Identity: The Stories of Japanese Returnees. *International Journal of Bilingual Education and Bilingualism, 3* (1), 1–18.

Kanno, Y. (2003). *Negotiating Bilingual and Bicultural Identities: Japanese Returnees Betwixt Two Worlds*. Mahwah, NJ: Lawrence Erlbaum.

Kaplan, A. (1993). *French Lessons: A Memoir*. Chicago: University of Chicago Press.

Kaplan, A. (1994). On Language Memoir. In A. Bammer (Ed.), *Displacements: Cultural Identities in Question* (pp. 59–70). Bloomington, IN: Indiana University Press.

Kinginger, C. (2004). Alice Doesn't Live Here Anymore: Foreign Language Learning and Identity Reconstruction. In A. Pavlenko & A. Blackledge (Eds.), *Negotiation of Identities in Multilingual Contexts* (pp. 219–42). Clevedon, UK: Multilingual Matters.

Kouritzin, S. (2000a). A Mother's Tongue. *TESOL Quarterly, 34* (2), 311–24.

Kouritzin, S. (2000b). Bringing Life to Research: Life History Research and ESL. *TESL Canada Journal, 17* (2), 1–35.

Kouritzin, S. (2000c). Immigration Mothers Redefine Access to ESL Classes: Contradiction and Ambivalence. *Journal of Multilingual and Multicultural Development, 21* (1), 14–32.

Kress, G. (2005). Gains and Losses: New Forms of Texts, Knowledge, and Learning. *Computers and Composition, 22* (1), 5–22.

Kress, G., & van Leeuwen, T. (1996). *Reading Images: The Grammar of Visual Design*. London: Routledge.

Kvale, S. (1996). *InterViews: An Introduction to Qualitative Research Interviewing*. Thousand Oaks, CA: Sage.

Kvale, S., & Brinkmann, S. (2009). *InterViews: Learning the Craft of Qualitative Research Interviewing*. Second edition. Los Angeles: Sage.

Labov, W. (1972). *Language in the Inner City: Studies in the Black Vernacular*. Philadelphia: University of Pennsylvania Press.

Lam, A. (2002). Language Policy and Learning Experience in China: Six Case Histories. *Hong Kong Journal of Applied Linguistics, 7* (2), 57–72.

Lantolf, J.P., & Pavlenko, A. (2001). (S)econd (L)anguage (A)ctivity Theory: Understanding Second Language Learners as People. In M.P. Breen (Ed.), *Learner Contributions to Language Learning* (pp. 141–58). London: Longman.

Lapadat, J.C. (2000). Problematizing Transcription: Purpose, Paradigm, and Quality. *International Journal of Social Research Methodology, 3* (3), 203–19.

Lee, J.S. (2006). Exploring the Relationship between Electronic Literacy and Heritage Language Maintenance. *Language Learning and Technology, 10* (2), 93–113.

Li, W. (2011). Multilinguality, Multimodality, and Multicompetence: Code- and Mode-Switching by Minority Ethnic Children in Complementary School. *Modern Language Journal, 95* (3), 370–84.

Lieblich, A., Tuval-Mashiach, R., & Zilber, T. (1998). *Narrative Research: Reading, Analysis, and Interpretation*. Thousand Oaks, CA: Sage.

Lim, H.-Y. (2002). The Interaction of Motivation, Perception, and Environment: One EFL Learner's Experience. *Hong Kong Journal of Applied Linguistics, 7* (2), 91–106.

Lincoln, Y.S. (1997). Self, Subject, Audience, Text: Living at the Edge, Writing in the Margins. In W.G. Tierney & Y.S. Lincoln (Eds.), *Representation and the Text: Re-framing the Narrative Voice* (pp. 37–55). Albany, NY: State University of New York Press.

Liu, Y., & Xu, Y. (2011). Inclusion or Exclusion? A Narrative Inquiry of a Language Teacher's Identity Experience in the 'New Work Order' of Competing Pedagogies. *Teaching and Teacher Education, 27* (3), 589–97.

Lo, A. (2009). Lessons about Respect and Affect in a Korean Heritage Language School. *Linguistics and Education, 20* (3), 217–34.

Loughran, J., & Russell, T. (2002). *Improving Teacher Education Practices through Self-Study.* London: Routledge.

Macalister, J. (2012). Narrative Frames and Needs Analysis. *System, 40* (1), 120–8.

Malcolm, D. (2004). An Arabic-Speaking English Learner's Path to Autonomy through Reading. In P. Benson & D. Nunan (Eds.), *Learners' Stories: Difference and Diversity in Language Learning* (pp. 69–82). Cambridge: Cambridge University Press.

Marx, N. (2002). Never Quite a 'Native Speaker': Accent and Identity in the L2—and the L1. *Canadian Modern Language Review, 59* (2), 264–81.

McKay, S., & Wong, S-L. (1996). Multiple Discourses, Multiple Identities: Investment and Agency in Second-Language Learning among Chinese Adolescent Immigrant Students. *Harvard Educational Review, 66* (3), 577–608.

Medgyes, P. (1994). *The Non-native Teacher.* London: Macmillan.

Menard-Warwick, J. (2004). "I Always Had the Desire to Progress a Little": Gendered Narratives of Immigrant Language Learners. *Journal of Language, Identity, and Education, 3* (4), 295–311.

Menezes, V. (2008). Multimedia Language Learning Histories. In P. Kalaja, V. Menezes, & A.M.F. Barcelos (Eds.), *Narratives of Learning and Teaching EFL* (pp. 199–213). Basingstoke, UK: Palgrave Macmillan.

Miles, M.B., & Huberman, A.M. (1994). *Qualitative Data Analysis: An Expanded Sourcebook.* Second edition. London: Sage.

Miller, E.R. (2011). Indeterminacy and Interview Research: Co-constructing Ambiguity and Clarity in Interviews with an Adult Immigrant Learner of English. *Applied Linguistics, 32* (1), 43–59.

Mishler, E.G. (1986). *Research Interviewing: Context and Narrative.* Cambridge, MA: Harvard University Press.

Murphey, T., & Carpenter, C. (2008). The Seeds of Agency in Language Learning Histories. In P. Kalaja, V. Menezes, & A.M.F. Barcelos (Eds.), *Narratives of Learning and Teaching EFL* (pp. 17–34). Basingstoke, UK: Palgrave Macmillan.

Murphey, T., Chen, J., & Chen, L-C. (2004). Learner's Constructions of Identities and Imagined Communities. In P. Benson & D. Nunan (Eds.), *Learners' Stories: Difference and Diversity in Language Learning* (pp. 83–100). Cambridge: Cambridge University Press.

Murray, G. (2004). Two Stories of Self-Directed Language Learning. In H. Reinders, H. Anderson, M. Hobbs, & J. Jones-Parry (Eds.), *Supporting Independent Learning in the 21st Century. Proceedings of the Inaugural Conference of the Independent Learning Association, Melbourne September 13–14 2003* (pp. 112–20). Auckland: Independent Learning Association Oceania.

Murray, G. (2008). Communities of Practice: Stories of Japanese EFL Learners. In P. Kalaja, V. Menezes, & A.M.F. Barcelos (Eds.), *Narratives of Learning and Teaching EFL* (pp. 128–40). Basingstoke, UK: Palgrave Macmillan.

Murray, G., & Kojima, M. (2007). Out-of-Class Learning: One Learner's Story. In P. Benson (Ed.), *Learner Autonomy 8: Insider Perspectives on Autonomy in Language Teaching and Learning* (pp. 25–40). Dublin: Authentik.

Nam, C., & Oxford, R.L. (1998). Portrait of a Future Teacher: Case Study of Learning Styles, Strategies, and Language Disabilities. *System, 26* (1), 51–63.

Nekvapil, J. (2003). Language Biographies and the Analysis of Language Situations: On the Life of the German Community in the Czech Republic. *International Journal of the Sociology of Language, 162*, 63–83.

Nelson, C.D. (2011a). Narratives of Classroom Life: Changing Conceptions of Knowledge. *TESOL Quarterly*, *45* (3), 463–85.

Nelson, C.D. (2011b). A Live Readers' Theatre Performance based on Classroom Research. Invited session, TESOL Convention, New Orleans, LA.

Nelson, C.D. (2013). From Transcript to Playscript: Dramatising Narrative Research. In G. Barkhuizen (Ed.), *Narrative Research in Applied Linguistics* (pp. 220–43). Cambridge: Cambridge University Press.

Nikula, T., & Pitkänen-Huhta, A. (2008). Using Photographs to Access Stories of Learning English. In P. Kalaja, V. Menezes, & A.M.F. Barcelos (Eds.), *Narratives of Learning and Teaching EFL* (pp. 171–85). Basingstoke, UK: Palgrave Macmillan.

Norrick, N.R. (2000). *Conversational Narrative: Storytelling in Everyday Talk*. Amsterdam: John Benjamins.

Norton, B. (2000). *Identity and Language Learning: Gender, Ethnicity and Educational Change*. London: Longman.

Norton, B. (2001). Non-participation, Imagined Communities, and the Language Classroom. In M. Breen (Ed.), *Learner Contributions to Language Learning: New Directions in Research* (pp. 159–171). Harlow, UK: Pearson Education.

Norton, B., & Toohey, K. (2001). Changing Perspectives on Good Language Learners. *TESOL Quarterly*, *35* (2), 307–22.

Nunan, D., & Choi, J. (Eds.). (2010). *Language and Culture: Reflective Narratives and the Emergence of Identity*. London: Routledge.

O'Móchain, R. (2006). Discussing Gender and Sexuality in a Context-Appropriate Way: Queer Narratives in an EFL College Classroom in Japan. *Journal of Language, Identity, and Education*, *5* (1), 51–66.

O'Sullivan, H. (2010). Autonomy Abroad: Metaphors of Mündigkeit in Language Learner Narrative. *Language and Intercultural Communication*, *10* (2), 106–8.

Ochs, E., & Capps, L. (2001). *Living Narrative: Creating Lives in Everyday Storytelling*. Cambridge, MA: Harvard University Press.

Ogulnick, K. (Ed.). (2000). *Language Crossings: Negotiating the Self in a Multicultural World*. New York: Teachers College Press.

Oxford, R.L. (1995). When Emotion Meets (Meta)cognition in Language Learning Histories. *International Journal of Educational Research*, *23* (7), 581–94.

Oxford, R.L. (2001). 'The Bleached Bones of a Story': Learners' Constructions of Language Teachers. In M.P. Breen (Ed.), *Learner Contributions to Language Learning: New Direction in Research* (pp. 86–111). London: Longman.

Pahl, K. (2004). Narrative, Artifacts and Cultural Identities: An Ethnographic Study of Communicative Practices in Homes. *Linguistics and Education*, *15* (4), 339–58.

Pavlenko, A. (1998). Second Language Learning by Adults: Testimonies of Bilingual Writers. *Issues in Applied Linguistics*, *9* (1), 3–19.

Pavlenko, A. (2001a). "How am I to Become a Woman in an American Vein?": Transformations of Gender Performance in Second Language Learning. In A. Pavlenko, A. Blackledge, I. Piller, & M. Teutsch-Dwyer (Eds.), *Multilingualism, Second Language Learning, and Gender* (pp. 133–73). Berlin: Mouton de Gruyter.

Pavlenko, A. (2001b). "In the World of the Tradition, I was Unimagined": Negotiation of Identities in Cross-cultural Autobiographies. *International Journal of Bilingualism*, *5* (3), 317–44.

Pavlenko, A. (2001c). Language Learning Memoirs as a Gendered Genre. *Applied Linguistics*, *22* (2), 213–40.

Pavlenko, A. (2002). Narrative Study: Whose Story is it, Anyway? *TESOL Quarterly*, *36* (2), 213–18.

Pavlenko, A. (2007). Autobiographic Narratives as Data in Applied Linguistics. *Applied Linguistics, 28* (2), 163–88.

Pietikäinen, S., Alanen, R., Dufva, H., Kalaja, P., Leppanen, S., & Pitkanen-Huhta, A. (2008). Languaging in Ultima Thule: Multilingualism in the Life of a Sami Boy. *International Journal of Multilingualism, 5* (2), 79–99.

Pink, S. (Ed.). (2012). *Advances in Visual Methodology.* London: Sage.

Polkinghorne, D.E. (1988). *Narrative Knowing and the Human Sciences.* Albany, NY: State University of New York Press.

Polkinghorne, D.E. (1995). Narrative Configuration in Qualitative Analysis. *Qualitative Studies in Education, 8* (1), 5–23.

Polkinghorne, D.E. (1997). Reporting Qualitative Research as Practice. In W.G. Tierney & Y.S. Lincoln (Eds.), *Representation and the Text: Re-framing the Narrative Voice* (pp. 3–21). Albany, NY: State University of New York Press.

Poon, A.Y.K. (2008). How Action Research Can Complement Formal Language Teacher Education. *The Asia-Pacific Education Researcher, 17* (1), 43–62.

Porter, J. (2002). Why Technology Matters to Writing: A Cyberwriter's Tale. *Computers and Composition, 20* (4), 375–94.

Propp, V. (1968). *The Morphology of the Folktale* (Translated by L. Scott. First published in Russian, 1928). Second Edition. Austin, TX: University of Texas Press.

Rajadurai, J. (2010). "Malays are Expected to Speak Malay": Community Ideologies, Language Use and the Negotiation of Identities. *Journal of Language, Identity, and Education, 9* (2), 91–106.

Reeves, J. (2009). A Sociocultural Perspective on ESOL Teachers' Linguistic Knowledge for Teaching. *Linguistics and Education, 20* (2), 109–25.

Reis, D.S. (2011). Non-native English-speaking Teachers (NNESTs) and Professional Legitimacy: A Sociocultural Theoretical Perspective on Identity Transformation. *International Journal of the Sociology of Language, 208,* 139–60.

Richards, K. (2003). *Qualitative Inquiry in TESOL.* Basingstoke, UK: Palgrave Macmillan.

Richards, K. (2009). Trends in Qualitative Research in Language Teaching since 2000. *Language Teaching, 42* (2), 147–80.

Richards, K. (2011). Using Micro-analysis in Interviewer Training: 'Continuers' and Interviewer Positioning. *Applied Linguistics, 32* (1), 95–112.

Riessman, C.K. (1993). *Narrative Analysis.* Newbury Park, CA: Sage.

Riessman, C.K. (2008). *Narrative Methods for the Human Sciences.* Los Angeles: Sage.

Roberts, B. (2002). *Biographical Research.* Buckingham, UK: Open University Press.

Roebuck, R. (2000). Subjects Speak Out: How Learners Position Themselves in a Psycholinguistic Task. In J. Lantolf (Ed.), *Sociocultural Theory and Second Language Learning* (pp. 79–95). Oxford: Oxford University Press.

Rose, G. (2012). *Visual Methodologies: An Introduction to Researching with Visual Materials.* Third edition. London: Sage.

Rugen, B.D. (2010). The Relevance of Narrative Ratifications in Talk-in-Interaction for Japanese Pre-service Teachers of English. *Narrative Inquiry, 20* (1), 62–81.

Sakui, K. (2002). Swiss Cheese Syndrome: Knowing Myself as a Learner and Teacher. *Hong Kong Journal of Applied Linguistics, 7* (2), 136–51.

Sataporn, S., & Lamb, M. (2004). Accommodation Zone: Two Learners' Struggles to Cope with a Distance Learning English Course. In P. Benson & D. Nunan (Eds.), *Learners' Stories: Difference and Diversity in Language Learning* (pp. 119–33). Cambridge: Cambridge University Press.

Schmidt, R. (1983). Interaction, Acculturation, and the Acquisition of Communicative Competence: A Case Study of an Adult. In N. Wolfson & E. Judd (Eds.), *Sociolinguistics and Language Acquisition* (pp. 137–74). Rowley, MA: Newbury House.

Selfe, C., & Ulman, H.L. (2013). *Digital Archive of Literacy Narratives*. Retrieved from http://daln.osu.edu/.

Shedivy, S.L. (2004). Factors that Lead Some Students to Continue the Study of Foreign Language Past the Usual 2 Years in High School. *System, 32* (1), 103–19.

Shen, F. (1989). The Classroom and the Wider Culture: Identity as a Key to Learning English Composition. *College Composition and Communication, 40* (4), 459–66.

Shin, S.J. (2010). "What about Me? I'm Not Like Chinese but I'm Not Like American": Heritage-language Learning and Identity of Mixed-heritage Adults. *Journal of Language, Identity, and Education, 9* (3), 203–19.

Shoaib, A., & Dörnyei, Z. (2004). Affect in Lifelong Learning: Exploring L2 Motivation as a Dynamic Process. In P. Benson & D. Nunan (Eds.), *Learners' Stories: Difference and Diversity in Language Learning* (pp. 22–41). Cambridge: Cambridge University Press.

Silverman, D. (2006). *Interpreting Qualitative Data: Methods for Analysing Talk, Text, and Interaction*. Third edition. London: Sage.

Simpson, J. (2011). Telling Tales: Discursive Space and Narratives in ESOL Classrooms. *Linguistics and Education, 22* (1), 10–22.

Smith, B. (2007). The State of the Art in Narrative Inquiry: Some Reflections. *Narrative Inquiry, 17* (2), 391–8.

So, S., with Domínguez, R. (2004). Emotion Processes in Second Language Acquisition. In P. Benson & D. Nunan (Eds.), *Learners' Stories: Difference and Diversity in Language Learning* (pp. 42–55). Cambridge: Cambridge University Press.

Stokoe, E., & Edwards, D. (2007). Story Formulations in Talk-in-Interaction. In M. Bamberg (Ed.), *Narrative—State of the Art* (pp. 69–79). Amsterdam: John Benjamins.

Swain, M., & Miccoli, L.S. (1994). Learning in a Content-Based, Collaboratively-Structured Course: The Experience of an Adult ESL Learner. *TESL Canada Journal, 12* (1), 15–28.

Takeuchi, O. (2003). What Can We Learn from Good Foreign Language Learners? A Qualitative Study in the Japanese Foreign Language Context. *System, 31* (3), 385–92.

Teutsch-Dwyer, M. (2001). (Re)constructing Masculinity in a New Linguistic Reality. In A. Pavlenko, A. Blackledge, I. Piller, & M. Teutsch-Dwyer (Eds.), *Multilingualism, Second Language Learning, and Gender* (pp. 175–98). Berlin: Mouton de Gruyter.

Thomas, W.I., & Znaniecki, F. (1919). *The Polish Peasant in Europe and America: Monograph of an Immigrant Group. Volume 3*. Boston: Richard G. Badger.

Thompson, P. (2000). *The Voice of the Past: Oral History*. Third edition. Oxford: Oxford University Press.

Thornborrow, J., & Coates, J. (Eds.). (2005). *The Sociolinguistics of Narrative*. Amsterdam: John Benjamins.

Tierney, W.G. (1997). Lost in Translation: Time and Voice in Qualitative Research. In W.G. Tierney & Y.S. Lincoln (Eds.), *Representation and the Text: Re-framing the Narrative Voice* (pp. 23–36). Albany, NY: State University of New York Press.

Toolan, M.J. (2001). *Narrative: A Critical Linguistic Introduction*. Second edition. London: Routledge.

Tse, L. (2000). Student Perceptions of Foreign Language Study: A Qualitative Analysis of Foreign Language Autobiographies. *The Modern Language Journal, 84* (1), 69–84.

Tsui, A.B.M. (2007). The Complexities of Identity Formation: A Narrative Inquiry of an EFL Teacher. *TESOL Quarterly, 41* (4), 657–80.

Umino, T. (2004). Learning a Second Language with Broadcast Materials at Home: Japanese Students' Long-Term Experiences. In P. Benson & D. Nunan (Eds.), *Learners' Stories: Difference and Diversity in Language Learning* (pp. 134–49). Cambridge: Cambridge University Press.

van Lier, L. (1988). *The Classroom and the Language Learner.* London: Longman.

Vandrick, S. (2009). *Interrogating Privilege: Reflections of a Second Language Educator.* Ann Arbor, MI: University of Michigan Press.

Vásquez, C. (2011). TESOL, Teacher Identity and the Need for 'Small Story' Research. *TESOL Quarterly, 45* (3), 535–45.

Vasudevan, L., Schultz, K., & Bateman, J. (2010). Rethinking Composing in a Digital Age: Authoring Literate Identities through Multimodal Storytelling. *Written Communication, 27* (4), 442–68.

Watson, C. (2007). Small Stories, Positioning Analysis, and the Doing of Professional Identities in Learning to Teach. *Narrative Inquiry, 17* (2), 371–89.

Webster, L., & Mertova, P. (2007). *Using Narrative Inquiry as a Research Method: An Introduction to Using Critical Event Narrative Analysis in Research on Learning and Teaching.* Abingdon, Oxon: Routledge.

Wenger, E. (1998). *Communities of Practice.* Cambridge: Cambridge University Press.

Wette, R., & Barkhuizen, G. (2009). Teaching the Book and Educating the Person: Challenges for University English Language Teachers in China. *Asia Pacific Journal of Education, 29* (2), 195–212.

Xu, Y., & Liu, Y. (2009). Teacher Assessment Knowledge and Practice: A Narrative Inquiry of a Chinese College EFL Teacher's Experience. *TESOL Quarterly, 43* (3), 493–513.

Yelenevskaya, M., & Fialkova, L. (2003). From 'Muteness' to 'Eloquence': Immigrants' Narratives about Languages. *Language Awareness, 12* (1), 30–48.

INDEX